DEOGRACIAS BILO

The effectiveness of air pollution control mechanisms

DEOGRACIAS BILO

The effectiveness of air pollution control mechanisms

International environmental law in search of efficient air protection.

ScienciaScripts

Cover image: www.ingimage.com

This book is a translation from the original published under ISBN 978-620-6-71705-8.

Publisher:
Sciencia Scripts
is a trademark of
Dodo Books Indian Ocean Ltd. and OmniScriptum S.R.L publishing group

120 High Road, East Finchley, London, N2 9ED, United Kingdom
Str. Armeneasca 28/1, office 1, Chisinau MD-2012, Republic of Moldova, Europe
Managing Directors: Ieva Konstantinova, Victoria Ursu
info@omniscriptum.com

Printed at: see last page
ISBN: 978-620-8-87313-4

Dedication

A My parents Célestin BILO and Constantine BOLOSO for your encouragement and spiritual support;

To my dearest wife Sarah BULUKUNGU BILO and my children Sublime-Bénite BILO; Splendide BILO and Deonelle BILO, you are my joy in life.

Acronyms and abbreviations

D.I.E: Droit international de l'environnement ;

I.C.J.: International Court of Justice;

C.J.U.E.: Court of Justice of the European Union;

W.C.E.: World Court of the Environment:

C.R.E: Cour régionale de l'environnement ;

CAFDHP: Cour africaine des droits de l'homme et des peuples (African Court of Human and Peoples' Rights); ECOWAS: Communauté économique des Etats de l'Afrique de l'Ouest (Economic Community of West African States);

UNFCCC: United Nations Framework Convention on Climate Change; GHG: Greenhouse Gases;

UN: United Nations

NGO: non-governmental organization

UNEP: United Nations Environment Programme;

EU: European Union;

CONTENTS

INTRODUCTION:

The environment is unique in that it cannot be approached in a compartmentalized manner. What happens in one place can have major repercussions in any other place relatively far from the place of origin. The effects of pollution or environmental degradation have a way of showing their ugly face in the most unlikely places. Consequently, they should be everyone's concern . [1]

To illustrate this, we need only look at the Trail smelter case, a case of air pollution whose source was in Canada, but whose repercussions were felt as far away as the U.S. (*The case originated in the activities of a smelter established in 1896 near Trail, British Columbia*).

Indeed, the Trail smelter arbitration award of March 11, 1941 laid the foundations of international environmental law. As early as the end of the 19th century, fumes emanating from a zinc and lead smelter located in Trail, Canada, some ten kilometers from the American border, raised the issue of transboundary pollution and compensation for damage caused from one State to another.

Ever since the international community first became aware of the need to protect the environment in the early 1970s, at the Stockholm Conference on the Human Environment, the protection of all forms of life and their habitats has been at the heart of environmental concerns [2]

Air pollution, first observed globally at the end of the last century, is an ancient phenomenon, largely of natural origin (volcanic eruptions, erosion.....). However, modern human activity has introduced substances into the atmosphere that are harmful to health and the environment[3] , making the living environment unsuitable. Air pollution is perceived as one of the major health risk factors.

Various reports provide ample evidence of the negative impact of air pollution. In 2006, for example, the French National Public Health Agency estimated that air

---

[1] Ghana Superior Court of Justice. Center for public interest law and Anor vs Tema oil Refinery. Trial No. E12/91/07, Korbiech J (Ghana), available atwww.cepil.org.gh/files/CEPIL vs.-TOR

[2] 1972 Stockholm Declaration on the Human Environment

[3] Laurence PRAT, Droit de l'air : Cadre international et Communautaire, April 2004, article available at https://www.techniques-ingenieur.fr/base-documentaite/archives-th12/archives-environnement tiagO/archives-1/droit-de-l-air-cadre-international-et-communautaire-g1510/

pollution was responsible for 48,000 deaths a year in France . [4]

In 2018, the WHO estimated that seven million people worldwide were dying because they breathed air overloaded with fine particles, including 4.2 million victims of outdoor air pollution and 3.8 million of indoor air pollution. 91% of the world's population is exposed daily to air containing high levels of pollutants[5] . A study published in March 2019 in the cardiology journal European Heart journal estimated the number of premature deaths worldwide at 8.8 million every year[6] . Note that this new estimate is twice as high as previous ones; it thus exceeds that of tobacco-related mortality, put at 7.2 million deaths in 2015 by the WHO.

This unfortunate assessment of the living environment in general prompts us to reflect on the situation, and calls into question the law to the highest degree. This raises the question of the role of the law in protecting the environment in general and, more specifically, what can the law do to combat air pollution? As we all know, the law is merely an instrument used by governments to regulate society and repress deviant behaviour that might harm both society and the environment.

Indeed, it would be pointless to set environmental standards based solely on the goodwill of those to whom they are addressed, and on a kind of self-limitation polluters potential. No legal system domestic or international is effective if it lacks sanctions, the means to compel subjects of the law to submit to it through coercive measures

The offence is necessarily accompanied by a panoply of measures designed to repress its commission and punish the perpetrator.

In the field of the environment, this is not an easy task, as the culprit is very often the State itself, either because of its laxity or shortcomings, or because of its activities carried out by administrations or companies for which it is the principal

[4] Laetitia van Eeck hourt, " la pollution de l'air est responsable de 9 % de la mortalité en France " available on : (https://www.lemonde.fr/pollution/article/2016/06/21/la-pollution-de-l-air-est-responsable-de-9-de-la- mortalité-en-France_4954518_1652666.html) , on le monde, June 21, 2016.

[5] Stéphane Mandard, "Air pollution kills 7 million people a year worldwide, WHO warns" Available at: (https://www.lemende.fr/planete/article/2018/05/02/la-pollution-de-l-air-tue-7-millions-de- personnes-par-an--dans-le-monde-allerte-l-oms_5293076_3244.html) le monde, May 2, 2018.

[6] Laiadi and alii. synergie entre pollens et polluants chimiques de l'air : les risks croisés (https://www.Jle.com/fr/revues/sante_pub/ers/e-docs/00/01/FB/D5/article.md?type=text.html) , Environnement, Risques& santé, vol.1,n°1, 42-9, mars-avril 2002, synthèses.

manager . [7]

Chapter 8 of the UN's Agenda 21, which deals with "integrating environmental and development decision-making", calls for the establishment of a legal framework at national level, while acknowledging that "laws and regulations adapted to the specific situation of each country are among the most important instruments for ensuring the implementation of environmental and development policies, not only because of their binding nature but also because of their normative effect on economic planning and market instruments" . [8]

This statement by Agenda 21 shows that the law is indeed one of the most important instruments for the success of an environmental policy[9] . It is in this sense that Professor Kamto points out that "law is inseparable from environmental protection, because it is closely linked to any form of protection"[10] . There can be no protection or prevention without prohibition or without prescribing behavior. Yet law, at least in its simplest form, is nothing other than a set of prohibitive or permissive prescriptions. This means that any desire for protection in the environmental field, as in any other, must necessarily be based on legal standards, i.e. binding rules. These standards may take the form of international conventions, national laws and regulations, or directives issued by international institutions . [11]

It can be deduced from the above analysis that environmental law also plays a dissuasive role. The law also acts as a deterrent to environmental damage, in the sense that a number of social actors, as Kamto points out, respect the law only out of fear of the penalties it entails; it is this fear that leads them to refrain from infringing the rules protecting the environment. So, for example, a law imposing a heavy penalty on anyone guilty of introducing or storing hazardous waste on national territory could have the effect of deterring those who might be tempted to commit such a forait. The same applies to air pollution.

The dissuasive dimension of environmental law is therefore designed to reinforce its anticipatory dimension, through the enactment of sanctions applicable in the event of non-compliance with anticipatory measures. In other words, the

---

[7] Mario Bettati, *International Environmental Law*, Odile Jacob, 2012, PP. 217-240

[8] Agenda 21, § 8.13

[9] Emmanuel D. Kan yogo, *manuel judiciaire de droit de l'environnement en Afrique*, Quebec, IFDD, 2018, P.2

[10] Maurice KAMTO, *Droit de l'environnement en Afrique*, Paris, Edicef/Aupelf, 1996, P.17

[11] Idem, P.17

dissuasive dimension makes it possible to punish or, simply, discipline individual or collective behaviour that does not comply with anticipatory prescriptions or proscriptions . [12]

International environmental law seeks to regulate the relationship between man and nature, by establishing rules for its protection and the protection of its habitat. *Hence the central question of this dissertation, which needs to be answered in terms of a contribution to this subject, is whether the repressive mechanisms set up by international environmental law to combat air pollution are effective and efficient. Can the norm be controlled or sanctioned? And how? By whom? If not, two subsidiary questions deserve to be raised: what would explain the ineffectiveness or low effectiveness and inefficiency of the repressive action against air pollution? How can the normative and institutional framework for optimal management of air pollution be made effective and efficient at both universal and regional levels*?

The notion of mechanism, pollution, effectiveness and efficiency will be developed in the following lines.

What enforcement mechanisms does international environmental law have at its disposal to deal with air pollution? An inventory of the normative and institutional framework will be examined below, to determine not only its effectiveness but also its efficiency. Such a study cannot fail to be of theoretical and practical interest.

Theoretically, the present study reviews a number of legal instruments and institutional mechanisms for combating air pollution in order to identify their strengths and weaknesses, while making a contribution de lege ferenda.

Indeed, the contribution is envisaged in the study of air pollution control mechanisms de lege lata (the law as it exists) and to consider proposals for their improvement in de lege ferenda (the law as it should be envisaged). A statement of the current state of affairs opens the way to de lege ferenda, which consists in examining the law with a view to improving it and introducing desirable legislative reforms.

While in ancient Rome, the law could only be kept alive if a jurisconsult improved it through his daily work, it must be admitted that to this day, the work of research and comparison by doctrinaires contributes to improving, harmonizing and

[12] Emmanuel D. Kan, op.cit. P.3

creating the law[13] . In the case under consideration, the aim is to understand the repressive mechanisms provided for at both universal and regional levels against air pollution.

On a practical level, while it's true that air provides a living environment, it must also be recognized that poor-quality air, or rather polluted air, means death. With this in mind, air quality is everyone's concern. The aspect of protection against the deterioration of air quality is a legal issue, as highlighted above, and consequently calls on jurists, legislators, institutional leaders, in particular magistrates, lawyers and other auxiliaries of justice, who will find food for thought in this study, where the future of our planet depends on it. Indeed, it would be wise to point out that, on the eve of the launch of the Paris conference (COP 21), the seriousness of climate and environmental change was neither disputable, nor indeed really disputed, with all the studies and reports, whether national, regional or global, drawn up from public or private sources, converging on the same, unequivocal observation: for several decades we have been witnessing the continuing deterioration of the general state of our planet[14] . This leads us to argue that other players, both international and national, will undoubtedly find in the present study a support that can help them to deepen their reflections on the subject.

Accordingly, the analysis in this dissertation will look first at the current state of air pollution control mechanisms in International Environmental Law (Part I), while also taking stock of the existing normative and institutional mechanisms in place in this field. We will demonstrate that, despite the multitude of different existing texts, they are not effective in meeting the expectations of their consecration. Our suggestions for the future (Part II)will contribute to a better understanding of air pollution in International Environmental Law, so that we can hope for a harmonious and legally secure living environment.

---

[13] Aser NZOVU LUVUJI, *prévention de la pollution de l'eau dans le Bassin du Congo : Evaluation et redéfinition des mécanismes régionaux et nationaux des Etats Fondateurs de la commission Internationale du Bassin du Congo-Oubangui-sangha (CICOS)*, PhD thesis in law, Université de KISANGANI, 2019-2020, P.12

[14] Rapport du club des juristes, *renforcer l'efficacité du droit International de l'environnement : devoirs des Etats, droits des* individus, November 2005, P.23

PART ONE: THE STATE OF PLAY OF AIR POLLUTION CONTROL MECHANISMS IN INTERNATIONAL ENVIRONMENTAL LAW

ENVIRONMENTAL LAW

Air pollution control mechanisms include legal instruments, actors, institutions and techniques. However, our study will only exceptionally refer to legal instruments and institutional mechanisms, leaving aside the other aspects of the mechanisms. We will inventory and describe these mechanisms at universal and regional level, in order to determine their effectiveness and, if necessary, their efficiency.

The scientific essay is underpinned by the concepts and expressions to be used, through their extension, nature, properties and characteristics. Effectiveness, mechanism, pollution, air and repression are, in our view, the key elements whose meaning, nature and extensions need to be identified.

The basis of this aspect is the fact that analysis and understanding of these concepts and expressions allows us to address concerns relating not only to the importance of these notions, but also, the meaning used insofar as, it is true, concepts and expressions are often polysemous. These expressions and concepts need to be used and situated within a theoretical framework appropriate to the subject matter.

Hence the structure of this part in two chapters, dealing respectively with the conceptual and theoretical framework (chapter I) and the low effectiveness of air pollution control mechanisms in D.I.E. (chapter II).

CHAPTER I. CONCEPTUAL AND THEORETICAL FRAMEWORK

The first chapter of this part deals with the clarification of essential notions and the theoretical framework. The point of this exercise is to fix minds on the meaning of these concepts (section 1) within the framework of this book. This will enable us to carry out critical analyses (section 2) of the mechanisms covered by the present analysis .

Section 1: Concept clarification

It is essential to clarify concepts before any development. The concepts whose meaning needs to be clarified are "mechanism" and "pollution" (§1) on the one hand, and "effectiveness" on the other (§2).

§1 Notion of mechanism and pollution

What should be understood by "mechanism" (1.1) and "pollution" (1.2)?

1.1. Understanding the word mechanism

The word mechanism refers to a device made up of parts assembled or connected to one another and fulfilling a given function. It can also mean a sequence of operations specific to a function. It is synonymous with an instrument used to achieve an objective.

Referring to the United Nations (UN) Practical Guide to Effective State Cooperation with International Human Rights Mechanisms, they dwell somewhat on the term national mechanism.

For the UN, a national reporting and monitoring mechanism is a national public structure or arrangement responsible for coordinating and preparing reports for international or regional human rights mechanisms and for collaborating with these mechanisms, as well as coordinating and monitoring the follow-up and implementation at national level of treaty obligations and recommendations emanating from these mechanisms . [15]

So how should we understand the term "mechanism"? In our view, a harmonious understanding of the words national and regional is in order.

[15] See in this sense, N.U, mécanismes nationaux d'élaboration des rapports et de suivi, guide pratique sur la collaboration efficace de l'Etat avec les mécanismes internationaux des droits de l'homme, New York and Geneva, 2016, P. 2

Indeed, the adjective national refers to what is relative to a Nation or a State. In other words, it refers to the internal structures of a state, while recalling that the modern state has internal sovereignty. From this sovereignty, it can organize its structures according to its own aspirations and expectations, with a view to achieving the objectives it sets itself.

It should therefore be noted that this principle of state sovereignty over its natural resources gives it full power to institute legal rules within its borders. By instituting rules in a sovereign manner, the State has the latitude to include legal rules of protection and will also exploit its sovereignty in the organization of an efficient and well-equipped administration to materialize its options in the field of the environment in general and pollution prevention in particular, as Aser NZOVU points out . [16]

Moreover, Raphael ROMI does not hesitate to include the environmental administration among the mechanisms for monitoring and controlling pollution . [17]

As Auguste MAMPUYA points out at[18] , the international world is currently experiencing universal, regional and even sub-regional state reporting. He points out that universalism and regionalism coexist. The universal level brings together all the world's states around universal values such as peace, human rights and the environment[19] . The UN is its standard-bearer. On the other hand, the particular interests of states on a given continent can also lead to groupings at this level. Such groupings are called regional. Such is the case of the African Union and the European Union. It follows that within regional groupings, states with common interests organize themselves to form sub-groups, often called sub-regional groupings.

To reflect this reality, the preamble to Agenda 21 states that
"in this context, the UN system has an essential role to play.

Other international, regional and sub-regional organizations should also contribute to this effort" . [20]

In the context of this text, the word regional refers to the study of the mechanisms put in place by the States of a region to prevent pollution.

Thus, the expression "mechanism" refers to all the arrangements put in place at

---

[16] Aser NZOVU LUVUJI, *Constitutionalisation du droit de l'eau et souveraineté des Etats: contribution pour une meilleure protection des ressources en eau*, éditions universitaires européennes, 2017, P. 47

[17] Raphaël ROMI, *Droit et Administration de l'Environnement*, 4^{e}édition, Montchrestien, EJA, Paris, 2001, P.56

[18] Auguste MAMPUYA Kanunk'a-Tshiabo, Traité de droit international public, Médiaspaul, Kinshasa, 2016, P. 115

[19] Aser NZOVU LUVUJI, Doctoral thesis, op.cit., P.50

[20] Agenda 21, op.cit.

both international (universal) and regional level to fulfil a specific role. In this case, the role in question is the suppression of air pollution. Resulting from a combination of several elements, the mechanisms of air pollution control include: the legal instruments, institutions, actors and techniques that contribute to this objective.

But what about the air itself?

There are hardly any means of depolluting and reprocessing air[21] . Air is one of the essential components of the environment, and just as indispensable for sustaining life on the planet. It is therefore a vital element.

The Congolese legislator defines "air" as "*the atmospheric layer enveloping the earth's surface, which is necessary for life, and whose physical, chemical or other modification may be harmful to the environment and to health*"[22] . Air is considered pure when its composition has a positive effect on man and nature. The quality of this resource is intimately linked to the quality of life.

For Bernard Drobenko, air quality is not just of interest to humans. He points out that air quality concerns all spaces and species, whether urban or rural, and requires a local, regional and international approach. It is now scientifically proven that deteriorating air quality has an impact on the biosphere, and is a source of disease and mortality. Numerous phenomena such as desertification, changes in the ozone layer, etc., are directly linked to the effects of human activities and the resulting air pollution . [23]

Protecting the air is therefore one of the imperatives that governments must take on in an attempt to maintain good living conditions on earth, even if some are still indifferent and believe that this is a speculation to slow down development.

It must be recognized that development only makes sense when it contributes to the quality of life of present generations, without compromising that of future generations. It must not only aim to satisfy their needs in quantity, but also in quality. To achieve this, preserving the quality of the environment, and more specifically of the air, is an essential prerequisite.

To see this, we need only look at Jean-Marc LAVIEILLE's immense cry of alarm on this subject, when he notes that "our Earth is not an uninhabitable furnace, unlike

---

[21] G. KALAMBAY LUMPUNGU and PAULIN MUNENE YAMBA-YAMBA, *Droit congolais de l'environnement*, édition Espérance, Paris, 2020, P. 309

[22] Article 2 point 1 of law n°11/009 of July 09, 2011 on the fundamental principles relating to environmental protection in the Democratic Republic of the Congo, Journal officiel-numéro spécial-July 16, 2011.

[23] Bernard Drobenko, *Droit international de l'environnement*, cours, option 2, droit comparé de l'environnement, le droit Français, partie 2 : *les pollutions, la lutte sectorielle : l'air*, Master 2, université de limoges, campus numérique, envidroit, P.3

the planet Venus, which is unliveable with air heated to 45°C." He goes on to say that Venus has tipped over into a massive greenhouse effect (95% C02), which has led to the evaporation of oceans, among other things. And yet, he continues, Venus has tipped over into a massive greenhouse effect (95% C02) that has led, among other things, to the evaporation of the oceans. On our planet, he argues, at the start of the 21st century, the problems, dramas and threats of global warming are underway. In the centuries to come, will the Earth become a Venus without living beings? he asks! [24]

Michel PRIEUR reveals that we have recently witnessed growing recognition of a human right to the environment, which can accompany the promotion of sustainable development. If the environment has acquired the status of a fundamental right, it is because it has become the expression of a public policy of collective interest, expressing new solidarities not only within States, but also on an international scale. Thus, he continues, there can be no sustainable development without respect for human rights, in particular the human right to the environment . [25]

Several legal instruments also convey this aspect. Indeed, the 1948 Universal Declaration of Human Rights refers to the right to life in Article 3 and the right to health in Article 25. The International Covenant on Civil and Political Rights proclaims the right to security (Article 9) and the 1966 Covenant on Economic, Social and Cultural Rights advocates the right to health (Article 12); the Strasbourg Resolution of the Institute of International Law of September 4, 1997 proclaims that "every human being has the right to live in a healthy environment" and that "the effective realization of the right to live in a healthy environment must be integrated into the objectives of sustainable development".

On the American continent, Article 11 of the Additional Protocol to the American Convention on Human Rights, dealing with economic, social and cultural rights, adopted in Sun Salvador on November 17 1988 and entered into force on November 16 1999, proclaims: "Everyone has the right to live in a healthy environment and to benefit from essential public services. States have an obligation to strengthen the protection, preservation and improvement of the environment".

Reports by the Inter-American Commission on Human Rights on certain countries have highlighted a direct link between the state of the environment and the

[24] Read Jean-Marc LAVIEILLE, *Droit international de l'environnement*, cours n°1, *l'air et les climats*, Master 2, université de limoges, campus numérique, envidroit, P.3

[25] Michel PRIEUR, Droit de l'environnement, Droit durable, Bruylant, 2013, P.297

fundamental rights to life and health. For example, the 1997 report on Ecuador highlights the dramatic effects of oil activities on water, *air* and health. Compliance with the American Convention for the Protection of Human Rights and Fundamental Freedoms, which protects the right to life and physical integrity, and Ecuador's 1998 Constitution, which entrusts the State with the task of guaranteeing the right to live in a healthy, ecologically balanced and pollution-free environment (article 23-6), should help improve the situation.

The report on Surinam notes that mercury released into the environment in the vicinity of indigenous communities constituted a permanent threat to the life, health and environment of these populations . [26]

The above development bears witness to the extent to which protecting the environment, and more particularly the air, is essential, not only for human life but also for the habitat in general, since its development depends on it.

And at African regional level, Article 24 of the African Charter on Human and Peoples' Rights proclaims that "all peoples have the right to a satisfactory and comprehensive environment conducive to their development".

To put it another way, a polluted environment or, better still, polluted air does nothing to promote life in all its various forms, because pollution is a nuisance and deserves to be punished. Hence the need to clarify the notion of pollution.

1.2. The notion of pollution

What do we mean by pollution in the context of this study, and is there a legal basis for this notion at both international and domestic level (a) ; what are its various sources (b) ?

a) Definition of pollution: the legal basis of the concept

As a reminder, the impetus for environmental protection came from the two Earth Summits, Stockholm 1972 and Rio 1992.

Raphael Romi considers that pollution is a reality that clearly determines conscious or unconscious actions that damage one or more natural elements that can be determined, identified and localized: *air pollution*, water pollution, soil pollution .[27]

According to serge Guinchard, pollution is the effect on land, water and the atmosphere of the dumping of waste, solid, liquid or gaseous residual products, and of the systematic use of chemical substances which, beyond a certain limit, quickly

[26] Michel PRIEUR, op.cit. P.303

[27] R. ROMI, op.cit. P. 10

destroy soil fertility after having enhanced it; also the effect of the imbalance in natural life, with the annihilation of certain classes of life (birds, insects, trees and plants), unable to resist the excess of sterilization and industrial dejecta[28] .

The notion of pollution is enshrined in a number of international and domestic legal instruments. Here are a few illustrations.

For the Beninese legislator, pollution is seen as "any contamination or direct or indirect modification of the environment caused by any act likely to adversely affect a use of the environment beneficial to man; to cause a situation prejudicial to the health, safety and well-being of man, flora and fauna, or to the safety of collective and individual property"[29] . For the Cameroonian legislator, pollution means "any contamination or direct or indirect modification of the environment caused by any act likely to adversely affect a use of the environment favorable to man; to cause or which is likely to cause a situation prejudicial to the health, safety, well-being of man, flora and fauna, *air*, atmosphere, water, soil and collective and individual property" . [30]

Congolese (DRC) and Togolese legislators have not remained silent on the issue. Indeed, for the former, the notion of pollution is perceived as being "a direct or indirect introduction, by human activity, of substances, vibrations, heat or noise into *the air*, water or soil, likely to harm health or the quality of the environment, to cause deterioration to material goods or to hinder the enjoyment of the environment or other legitimate uses of the latter"[31] . In contrast to previous notions of pollution, the Congolese legislator's text directly identifies the originator of pollution, attributing it directly to human activity.

For the latter, notably the Togolese legislator, pollution is "Any contamination or direct or indirect modification of the environment caused by an act likely to have a negative influence on the living environment of man and other living species; to cause a situation prejudicial to the health, safety and well-being of man, flora and fauna, or collective and individual property" . [32]

According to article 1 of the Côte d'Ivoire Environmental Code, pollution "is the direct or indirect contamination or modification of the environment by any act

[28] Serge Guinchard et alii, lexique des termes juridiques, 25ᵉédition, Dalloz, 2017-2018, P.1551.

[29] Read article 2 of law no. 98-030 of February 12, 1998 on the framework law on the environment in the Republic of Benin.

[30] Article 4 point V of law no. 96/12 of August 5, 1996 on the framework law for environmental management in Cameroon.

[31] This notion is provided for in article 32 of law n° 11/009 of July 09 2011, op.cit.

[32] This definition is proclaimed by article 2 point 40 of law no. 2008-005 of May 30, 2008 on the framework law on the environment in Togo.

likely to alter the living environment of man and other living species; to harm the health, safety and well-being of man, flora and fauna, or collective and individual property".

Jean-Pierre Beurier points out that the definition of pollution was established after some trial and error with the recommendation adopted by the OECD Council on November 14, 1974 (c C74) 224) proclaiming principles concerning transfrontier pollution: "...pollution is defined as the introduction by man, directly or indirectly, of substances or energy into the environment, resulting in adverse consequences of such a nature as to endanger human health, harm living resources and ecological systems, impair amenities or interfere with other legitimate uses of the environment"[33].

In the light of the definitional reading of pollution given above, it follows that air pollution is the voluntary or accidental emission into the atmospheric layer of gases or substances of such a nature as to create nuisances for living beings, to compromise their health or public safety, or to harm agricultural production and ecosystems - in short, the environment.

According to Nicolas de sadeleer, there are two possible approaches to pollution: pollution due to the transgression of a norm, and pollution due to the impact of the emission on the environment. In the first view, pollution is distinguished from environmental damage by its prohibited nature. In other words, not every emission constitutes pollution. In order to be considered pollution, the substance released into the environment must exceed the discharge or quality standards set by the public authorities. The concept of pollution thus depends on the transgression of a standard.

On the other hand, according to the opposing view, pollution is less a matter of violating a discharge threshold than of the nuisance caused by the substance to the environment or its victims[34]. In any case, this seems to be the viewpoint of international institutions, as confirmed by an analysis of the normative texts and recommendations of international law. Our point of view is a function of this definitional approach in the examination of this study.

b) <u>Sources of pollution</u>

Pollution is the main result of human activity. Man is at the heart of pollution.

---

[33] Jean-Pierre BEURIER, *Droit international de l'environnement*, édition A. Pedone, 2017, P. 133

[34] Nicolas de sadeleer, *les principes du pollueur-payeur, de prévention et de précaution, essai sur la genèse et la portée juridique de quelques principes du droit de l'environnement*, AUPELF-UREF, Bruylant Bruxelles, 1999, P. 71

Air quality concerns all species and areas, whether urban or rural, and requires a local, regional and international approach.

Bernard Drobenko points out that the sources of air pollution are varied: around 50% of pollution comes from domestic sources, 25% from industrial sources, and 25% from automobiles . [35]

Two theories can be applied to this study: pollution prevention theory and evaluation theory. The latter will be examined in the second part of this work, with a view to assessing the relevance of the inventory of air pollution control mechanisms examined in this first part.

Prevention consists in preventing environmental damage by taking appropriate preventive measures before a plan is drawn up or a work or activity carried out. Preventive action is an anticipatory and a priori action that has long been preferred to a posteriori measures such as repair, restoration or repression, which take place after a proven damage to the environment . [36]

The principle of prevention makes it possible to integrate environmental requirements right from the design phase of a project, and to guarantee that these requirements will be taken into account during the design, preparation and execution phases of a project.

The UN Convention on the Law of the Sea of December 10, 1982, for example, stipulates that where there are "serious reasons to believe that activities [...] are likely to cause significant pollution. States shall evaluate. as far as possible. the potential effects of such activities".

In his Essai de systématisation du principe de prévention, Nicolas de Sadeleer acknowledges that, by their number and diversity, the legal instruments that characterize the preventive function of environmental law give the principle of prevention a particularly variegated appearance[37] . In application, several types of prevention can be distinguished, including dissuasive prevention.

The word "dissuasive" is the feminine form of the qualifying adjective whose masculine form has the ending "if". It is therefore the feminine form of dissuasive.

As such, the adjective dissuasive means dissuading, in other words, something whose property is to dissuade someone or something. To dissuade can

---

[35] Bernard Drobenko, op.cit. P.1

[36] Michel PRIEUR, *les principes généraux du droit de l'environnement*, campus numérique, envidroit, université de limoges, Master 2, cours n° 5, P.31

[37] Nicolas de Sadeleer, op.cit. P. 114

mean to divert from the execution of a purpose or resolution.

Pierre-Marie Dupuy notes that "international liability for environmental damage is the last chance left when we have failed to protect degraded ecology. In other words, it's a last resort. When it comes to the environment, perhaps more than anywhere else, prevention is better than cure. Because when we heal, we still don't heal. The main advantage of liability as a legal institution is its dissuasive and therefore preventive character. If states know they are exposed to sanctions or obligations to make reparation, they will be encouraged to stop polluting" . [38]

Deterrent prevention is a set of measures designed to deter polluters from damaging the environment through the fear of administrative, civil or criminal sanctions. Normally, a sanction is imposed on a subject of law after the fact, i.e., after he or she has committed an act. Sanctions are applied to facts that have already occurred.

In principle, sanctions are part of the curative paradigm of environmental protection. Its prevention does not concern cases that have already occurred, but rather future cases. It is organized around civil liability, environmental liability, administrative liability and criminal liability . [39]

The development of this point being indicative, is not intended to go into depth on the question. Readers may wish to consult the relevant sources for further information.

The fight against air pollution is governed by international regulations. If we are to achieve a healthy environment, it is essential that the protection mechanisms put in place under the EIA are effective and meet the expectations of their consecration with efficiency.

Before going any further into the analysis of these mechanisms, we would like to focus on the concept of "effectiveness" in the context of this study.

§ 2 <u>Terminological framework for the concept of "effectivity</u>

First and foremost, we need to clarify the concept of effectivity. The noun "effectivity" does not appear as such in dictionaries. It refers to the real and concrete nature of a right, beyond its abstract recognition in legal texts. The right of access to a

[38] On this subject, see Pierre-Marie Dupuy, in video-cassette distance learning materials, in particular cassette no. 9, theme "International environmental responsibility", edited by J.M. Breton, AUPELF-UREF/video scope Nancy, 1998.

[39] Aser NZOVU LUVUJI, PhD thesis, op.cit. PP. 77-78

judge, for example, is only effective if the indigent litigant receives legal aid . [40]

In other words, it designates the character of what is "effective", i.e. what is done, what has a real and concrete effect, what exists in fact. For a right to be "effective", it must be translated into facts, i.e. into reality. The effectiveness of a right would be its concretization in fact. However, it is not a question of the primacy of fact over law, but of the translation of law into fact. This is feasible law.

In more legal terms, we would say that it is law that is applied, implemented and produces effects. Alongside the law on paper, the "formal law", we are interested in the law that is applied, the "real law". Effectiveness could be considered in its legal sense, as the meeting of law and fact, which ideally leads to their unity. A living right is a right that applies, as opposed to the obsolescence that characterizes a right that has become dead. A living law is one that is not only still in force, but also equipped with the legal means to enable it to be applied, monitored and, if necessary, sanctioned. Thus, the effectiveness of law requires a chain of components to go from law (the text) to fact (its application).

In the final analysis, the effectiveness of law is an obvious and banal requirement: law is made to be applied. But the effectiveness of the law first implies that the rule exists, that it is legally applicable, that it is respected, applied and controlled, and that it is eventually sanctioned by the administration and by the judge . [41]

Julien Bétaille draws a distinction between state-effectiveness and action-effectiveness. Effectiveness-state, he continues, is that which exists in reality, and effectivity-action, that which produces an effect on reality[42] . State-effectiveness would correspond to the meaning historically given by international law to effectivity, i.e. the legal assessment of a fact such as the occupation of a territory or a naval blockade. International law observes a fact and deduces from it the effectiveness of the fact observed, which leads to a legal qualification or a legal consequence. In classical international law, the fact creates the law.

Effectiveness-action, on the other hand, is the expression of law in action, i.e. the effects of law on the ground, manifested in obedience to the law. This would apply

[40] Serge Guinchard, op.cit. P.851

[41] Michel PRIEUR, *Les indicateurs juridiques. Outils d'évaluation de l'effectivité du droit de l'environnement*, Institut de la Francophonie pour le développement durable (IFFD), Québec, 2018, P. 7

[42] J. Bétaille, *les conditions juridiques de l'effectivité de la norme en droit interne : illustrations en droit de l'urbanisme et de l'environnement*, Thesis directed by Michel Prieur, University of Limoges, 2012, P.2, quoted by Michel Prieur, op.cit. P. 8

to domestic law. In this case, effectivity has a practical vocation insofar as it aims to assess the degree to which the law is applied in society. [43]

In reality, effectivity-state and effectivity-action are two sides of the same coin. While the former makes it possible to characterize the historical forms of effectivity in international law, it does not exclude effectivity-action to characterize international law.

Indeed, it is important to distinguish between effectiveness and efficacy, as the objectives and methods of evaluation are different.

The effectiveness of a rule of law in general is what is most commonly sought. A rule of law is considered relevant if it is effective, i.e. if it is socially useful in achieving its stated objective. This is the impact of a rule on society. This means that it must contribute to achieving a result that lies outside the legal system.

The examination of the law's effectiveness, on the other hand, takes place within the legal system. Effectiveness is therefore assessed in relation to the aim and objective pursued by the legal norm. The objective may be partially or fully achieved. Effectiveness, like efficacy, can therefore be relative.

An air law that sets pollution abatement levels to be achieved will be effective if the scientifically-measured abatement level is actually achieved. To reiterate the distinction made above, we are referring here only to the state-effectiveness: the concrete, material effect of the legal rule evaluated in the field. Effectiveness therefore measures whether the legal norm has achieved its objective(s). Effectiveness can be seen as a necessary but not sufficient condition for efficiency. [44]

It is worth noting that the theme of legal effectiveness is attracting growing interest from researchers and decision-makers alike. There has been a recent trend towards the "juridification" of the requirement for legal rules to be effective, reflected both in the particular attention paid to specific procedures for controlling or promoting standards or mechanisms for achieving conformity, and in the use of terms emphasizing the role of effectiveness, which has become a component of legal discourse. [45]

As a result, environmental law texts also expressly refer to the need for

---

[43] F. Rangeon, *réflexion sur l'effectivité du droit, in CURAPP, les usages sociaux du droit*, Paris, Presses universitaires de France, 1989, P.128, quoted by J. Bétaille, op.cit., P. 15.

[44] Michel PRIEUR, idem, P. 11

[45] A. Jeammaud, "*le concept d'effectivité*", in l'effectivité du droit du travail, à quelles conditions? P. 45-46, quoted by Michel PRIEUR, idem, P.12

effectiveness. Just look at the number of times the word "effectiveness" is used, as in the 1992 Rio Declaration.

Furthermore, the recent World Declaration on the Rule of Environmental Law, adopted in Rio de Janeiro on April 29, 2016 by the IUCN World Congress on the initiative of its World Commission on Environmental Law , clearly shows that judges and the community of environmental lawyers are now convinced that the future of environmental law depends on its effectiveness.

In this Declaration, the "effective" application of the law is called for seven times in a four-page text. In particular, it calls for the effective application of laws and regulations, and the creation of innovative legal tools for compliance and effective implementation.

Having clarified the concepts and expressions used, it is now time to analyze the existing normative and institutional framework for combating air pollution in France. This is the subject of the following section.

Section 2. Critical analysis of DIE's existing normative and institutional framework for combating air pollution.

Any control program, whether repressive or preventive, relies on a number of mechanisms tailored to the action and results to be achieved, as described by Leroy Yann[46] . With this in mind, an inventory of air pollution control mechanisms, especially legal instruments (§1) and the institutional mechanism "allusion made to the jurisdictional instance" (§2), is essential to the examination of the present section.

§ 1 Normative framework: legal instruments

As we have already noted, the United Nations (UN) conferences were the starting point for the international drive to protect the air. Indeed, the first UN conference on the human environment was held in Stockholm, Sweden, in 1972, and is considered by many authors to be the birth of international environmental law.

It should be noted that this conference ensured the environment a permanent place in a global action plan leading to the creation of the United Nations Environment Program (UNEP).

The participants adopted a declaration of 26 principles and a vast action plan to combat pollution.

---

[46] Leroy Yann, la notion d'effectivité du droit. Available at https://www.cairn.info/revue-droit-et- société1-2011-3-page-715.htm

Since this 1972 conference, a number of international agreements have been signed on environmental matters:

- ***the Geneva Convention of November 13, 1979 on Long-Range Transboundary Pollution***.

There are eight protocols to this Geneva Convention, including :

- ✓ Protocol on the Reduction of Emissions from the Cooperative Programme for Monitoring and Evaluation of the Long-range Transmission of Air Pollutants in Europe (EMEP), done at Geneva on September 28, 1984;
- ✓ Protocol on the reduction of sulphur emissions or their transboundary fluxes by at least 30%, done at Helsinki on July 8th 1985;
- ✓ Protocol concerning the Control of Emissions of Nitrogen Oxides or their Transboundary Fluxes, done at Sofia on October 31, 1988;
- ✓ Protocol concerning the control of emissions of volatile organic compounds or their transboundary fluxes, done at Geneva on November 18, 1991;
- ✓ Protocol on Further Reduction of Sulphur Emissions, done at Oslo on June 14, 1994;
- ✓ Protocol on Heavy Metals, done at Aarhus (Denmark) on June 24 1998;
- ✓ Protocol on Persistent Organic Pollutants, done at Aarhus on June 24 1998 and finally ;
- ✓ The Protocol to Abate Acidification, Eutrophication and Ground-level Ozone (Gothenburg Protocol), done at Gothenburg (Sweden) on November 30, 1999 . [47]

Article 1(b) of the Geneva Convention of November 13 1979 states that "long-range transboundary air pollution means air pollution whose physical source is wholly or partly within an area under the national jurisdiction of one State and which exerts harmful effects in an area under the jurisdiction of another State in such a way that it is generally not possible to distinguish the contributions of individual sources or groups of emission sources".

According to Professor Alexandre KISS, the Convention was "...the first major

[47] Texts available at https://www.unece.org/env/environnement-conventions.html

international treaty devoted to air pollution control which had just come into being" . [48]

One of the aims of the Convention is to protect man and the environment against air pollution, while endeavouring to limit as far as possible the reduction and prevention of air pollution.

It should be noted, however, that this convention does not contain any provisions relating to State liability for damage. The convention is of a programmatic nature, based on cooperation between the parties.

Article 6 of the said Convention stipulates that "taking into account Articles 2 to 5, ongoing research, exchange of information and monitoring activities and their results, the cost and effectiveness of local remedial and other measures, and to combat air pollution, in particular that arising from new or converted installations, each contracting party undertakes to develop the best policies and strategies, including *air quality* management systems and, within such systems, control measures, consistent with balanced development, using in particular the best available and economically feasible technology and techniques which produce little or no waste.

In the event of a dispute arising between two or more contracting parties to the present Convention as to the interpretation or application of the said Convention, the latter shall refer the parties concerned to an amicable settlement by negotiation or by any other method of dispute settlement acceptable to them.

- ***The Bamako Convention on the Ban of the Import Into Africa of Hazardous Wastes and on the Control of Transboundary Movements and Management of Hazardous Wastes Produced in Africa***

in Africa

This legal instrument was adopted on January 30, 1991 in Bamako and came into force on April 22, 1998. One of its general obligations is for the parties to take legal, administrative and other measures within their jurisdiction to prohibit the import into Africa of all hazardous wastes, for whatever reason, from non-contracting parties.

Such imports are declared illegal and subject to special penalties[49] . This prohibition is based on the determination of the parties to protect, through strict control, the human health of African populations and the environment against the

---

[48] KISS Alexandre, *la convention sur la pollution atmosphérique transfrontière à longue distance*, Revue juridique de l'environnement, n° 1, 1985, PP. 30-35

[49] This aspect is covered by Article 4 of the Bamako Convention under review.

harmful effects that may result from the production of hazardous waste. Indeed, the production and transboundary traffic of hazardous wastes often have a very negative impact on the environment, leading to pollution of the air and the ecosystem in general, without prejudice to the consequences that may result.

For the purposes of this Convention, Article 2 considers as hazardous wastes: wastes which belong to one of the categories listed in Annex I to this Convention; wastes to which the provisions of paragraph (a) above do not apply, but which are defined or considered as hazardous by the domestic legislation of the State of operation, import or transit; wastes which possess one of the characteristics listed in Annex II to this Convention;

Hazardous substances which have been banned, cancelled or refused registration by the regulatory actions of governments, or whose registration has been voluntarily withdrawn in the country of production for reasons of protection of human health or the environment; wastes which, because of their radioactivity, are subject to international control systems, including international instruments applying specifically to radioactive materials, are included in the scope of this convention.

It should also be noted that the Bamako and Basel Conventions also cover waste definitions, and are both based on prohibition and control.

The second conference of the parties to the Bamako Convention on the Ban of the Import into Africa of Hazardous Wastes, the Control of Transboundary Movements and the Management of Hazardous Wastes generated in Africa, which opened on January 30, 2018 under the theme "A fit planet for a pollution-free Africa"[50], bears witness to how much more considerable the fight against pollution is with a view to preserving human health in particular and the environment in general.

Through this convention, the parties undertake to enforce the obligations of the present convention and to prosecute the perpetrators of violations in accordance with their national legislation and/or international law[51]. As is well known, the purpose of recourse to the courts by a party is the adoption or pronouncement of a sanction by the judge, whatever its nature.

In terms of supervision (control), the parties designate a national body to act as a supervisory body. In this capacity, it will be called upon to coordinate with the

---

[50] Séverine NADAUD, *droit international de l'environnement, les déchets*, cours n° 6, option 1, université de limoges, Master 2, campus numérique, envidroit, P. 18

[51] This commitment is provided for in Article 4, a of the said Bamako Convention in connection with the general obligations of the Convention.

governmental and non-governmental bodies concerned.

Furthermore, it should be noted that the present convention, in relation to sanctions, refers this question to the parties. For example, Article 9(2) on illicit traffic in wastes stipulates that "each Party shall adopt appropriate national legislation to impose penal sanctions on any person who plans, carries out or collaborates in such illicit imports.

These sanctions must be sufficiently severe to punish such actions and have a preventive effect. The Convention also provides for recourse to arbitration by an ad hoc body set up by the Conference of the Parties for this purpose, or to the International Court of Justice, failing resolution by negotiation or by any other peaceful means of their choice, of any dispute arising between parties as a result of the interpretation, application or observance of the present Convention or any Protocol thereto . [52]

- **Protocol to the Espo Convention on Environmental Impact Assessment in a Transboundary Context concerning strategic environmental assessment**

This text was adopted on May 21, 2003 in Kiev and came into force on July 11, 2010. Under this legal instrument, the environmental impact, including health impacts, is taken into account. Indeed, Article 2, point 7, refers to it as "any effect on the environment, including human health, flora, fauna, biological diversity, soil, climate, ***air***, water, landscape, natural sites, material assets, cultural heritage and the interaction between these factors".

- **The Kyoto Protocol: an international instrument to combat climate change.**

This instrument came into force on February 16, 2005. It is an essential extension of the Framework Convention on Climate Change. It recognizes the existence of climate change, and in particular its human origins.

The protocol tackles greenhouse gas emissions, notably carbon dioxide (Co2), methane (CH4), nitrous oxide (N20), hydrofluorocarbons (HFCs), perfluorocarbons (PFCS) and sulfur hexafluoride (SF6).

The environmental consequences of these emissions include air pollution. This text advocates emission reductions by the States parties, by assessing their capacity to produce GHGs (Greenhouse Gases) on the one hand, and to compensate for these emissions on the other.

[52] Read article 20 of the convention.

This protocol is based on the United Nations Framework Convention on Climate Change, as mentioned above. The aim of the latter is to stabilize greenhouse gas concentrations in the atmosphere at a level that would prevent dangerous anthropogenic interference with the climate system.

In 2015, it was followed by the Paris Agreement. The latter (Paris Agreement) is an international agreement within the meaning of the Vienna Convention on the Law of Treaties.

As such, it is binding on the parties. On the other hand, sanctions have not been defined.

Indeed, the United Nations Framework Convention (UNFCCC) is based on an ultimate objective and any related legal instruments that the Conference of the Parties may adopt, that of stabilizing, in accordance with the relevant provisions of the Convention, greenhouse gas concentrations in the atmosphere at a level that would prevent dangerous anthropogenic interference with the climate system . [53]

According to the provisions of Article 3 of the Convention, the Parties are obliged to preserve the climate system for the benefit of present and future generations of humankind, on the basis of equity and in accordance with their common but differentiated responsibilities and respective capabilities; to take precautionary measures to anticipate, prevent or mitigate the causes of climate change and to limit its adverse effects [...].

These regulatory measures to be taken by the parties in relation to emissions of gaseous effluents ***into the air*** are in particular to contribute to maintaining good air quality by avoiding all forms of pollution.

Stockholm Convention Stockholm Convention on persistent organic pollutants

The Stockholm Convention on Persistent Organic Pollutants was adopted on May 22nd 2001 in Stockholm and entered into force on May 17th 2004, through which the parties recognize that persistent organic pollutants possess toxic properties, resist degradation, accumulate in living organisms and are transported by ***air***, water and migratory species across international boundaries and deposited far from their site of origin, where they accumulate in terrestrial and aquatic ecosystems.

In accordance with the provisions of articles 5 and 6, the parties are thus called upon to take measures to reduce or eliminate releases resulting from

[53] On this subject, read Article 2 of the UNFCCC of May 9, 1992, which came into force on March 21, 1994.

unintentional production, as well as releases from stockpiles and wastes.

To this end, each Party is called upon to encourage the development and, where it deems appropriate, require the use of substitute or modified materials, products and processes to prevent the formation and release of the chemicals listed in Annex C, taking into account the general guidelines on release prevention and reduction measures contained in Annex C as well as guidelines to be adopted by decision of the Conference of the Parties [...].

The Conference of the Parties shall develop and approve, as soon as practicable, procedures and institutional mechanisms for determining cases of non-compliance with the provisions of this Convention and the measures to be taken in respect of offending Parties. This is what Article 17 of the Convention stipulates.

It should also be noted that a European ambition in terms of air quality standards has been clearly assumed since 1993. On January 1, 1993, the European Council decided to implement a Community program of policy and action on the environment and sustainable development, with a view to health protection.

This led to the adoption of two directives considered to give fresh impetus to the fight against (atmospheric) ***air pollution***:

- ✓ Directive 96/62/EC of September 17, 1996 on ambient *air* quality assessment and management;
- ✓ Council Directive 1999/30/EC of April 22, 1999 relating to limit values for sulfur dioxide, nitrogen dioxide and oxides of nitrogen, particulate matter and lead in ambient *air*.

To these two initial texts, it is important to add other directives, which in the early 2000s completed the European arsenal for combating air pollution through emission limit values:

- ✓ Directive 2000/69/EC of the European Parliament and of the Council of November 16, 2000 relating to limit values for benzene and carbon monoxide (for 2010 and 2005 respectively) in ambient *air*;
- ✓ Directive 2001/81/EC of the European Parliament and of the Council of October 23, 2001 on national emission ceilings for certain *atmospheric* pollutants, in this case acidifying and eutrophying pollutants and ozone precursors;
- ✓ Directive 2002/3/EC of the European Parliament and of the Council of February 12, 2002 on ozone in ambient air;

- ✓ Directive 2004/107/EC of February 15, 2004 of the European Parliament and of the Council polycyclic aromatics in ambient air . [54]

  Added to the list :
- ✓ Directive 2008/50 of May 21, 2008 on *air quality*
- ✓ Directive (U.E) 2015/2193 of the European Parliament and of the Council of November 25, 2015 on the limitation of emissions of certain pollutants into the air from medium-sized combustion plants;
- ✓ Regulation (U.E) 2019/631 of the European Parliament and of the Council of April 17, 2019 setting CO2 emission performance standards for new passenger cars and light-duty vehicles, and repealing Regulations (EC) No 443/2009 and (EC) No 510/2011.

The European Union is a party to the Gothenburg Protocol, which amended the 1979 Geneva Convention on Long-Range Transboundary Air Pollution in 1999.

The rights of European citizens with regard to air quality include the right to be informed by EU institutions and the right to be protected by national and EU courts.

The adoption of Directive 2008/50/EC of May 21, 2008 is ample proof of this. Indeed, this text sets air quality objectives for all States, and requires them to assess air quality, take the necessary measures to maintain and improve it, and inform the public.

The threats to air quality are numerous. We have therefore reviewed a number of legal instruments of universal and regional scope.

Some of these instruments do not deal specifically with air pollution, but they do impose a general obligation on States to cooperate in protecting the environment in areas beyond national sovereignty, and they also include other environmental provisions relevant to air protection.

While States have the sovereign right to exploit their natural resources in accordance with their environmental policy, they are obliged to do so in compliance with this obligation.

In terms of consequences, a state that fails to meet its obligation to protect and preserve air quality would be in breach of the relevant rules of international law.

The violation of a rule of law calls for the sanctioning of the perpetrator of the infringement (in this case, the perpetrator would be called the polluter), so as to engage his responsibility.

---

[54] See report n° 610 of the French Senate, extraordinary session of 2014-2015, deposit published in the official journal, editions of laws and decrees of July 09, 2015 on page 39.

Nicolas de Sadeleer explains that the "polluter pays" principle has gradually established itself as a pillar of Community environmental policy, which quickly followed the recommendations adopted by the OECD Council by spelling out its content in a series of recommendations and resolutions, and subsequently conferring normative scope on it.

This principle was evoked for the first time in the first environmental action program (1973-1976), according to which the costs of preventing and eliminating nuisances are normally borne by the polluters.

on polluters[55] . Exceptions to these principles could only be accepted if they did not result in major distortions to international trade and investment.

According to Recommendation 75/436, "the natural and legal persons, whether under private or public law, responsible for pollution must pay the costs of the measures necessary to avoid or reduce such pollution in order to comply with the standards and equivalent measures enabling quality objectives to be attained or, where such objectives do not exist, in order to comply with the standards and equivalent measures laid down by the public authorities".

The polluter is defined as the person who "*directly or indirectly degrades the environment or creates conditions leading to its degradation*"[56] . The Congolese legislator considers the polluter to be the natural or legal person responsible for pollution, the latter (pollution) being understood as the direct or indirect introduction, by human activity, of substances, vibrations, heat or noise into the air [...] likely to harm health or the environment [...]. [57]

In other words, the "polluter pays" principle has had a significant influence on the development of national law, insofar as several countries have recognized it as a guiding principle of their environmental policy. This is notably the case in French law, which defines it as the principle "whereby the costs resulting from measures to prevent, reduce and combat pollution must be borne by the polluter" . [58]

Liability is set out in Principle 13 of the 1992 Rio Declaration on the Human Environment and Development, which states that "States shall develop national legislation concerning liability for pollution damage and other environmental harm, and for compensation of victims ; they must also cooperate diligently and more

---

[55] Nicolas de Sadeleer, op.cit. P.57

[56] Idem

[57] Article 2 point 31 et 32 de la loi portant principes fondamentaux relatifs à la protection de l'environnement en République Démocratique du Congo, op.cit.

[58] Article L 200-1 du nouveau code rural cited by Nicolas de sadeleer, op.cit. P.62

resolutely to develop new measures under international law concerning liability and compensation for the harmful effects of environmental damage caused by activities within their jurisdiction or control in areas beyond their jurisdiction".

Speaking of State liability, Pierre-Marie Dupuy points out that "The main advantage of liability as a legal institution is that it acts as a deterrent. If states know that they are exposed to sanctions or obligations to make reparation, they will be encouraged to stop polluting" .[59]

According to Aser Nzovu, the reality presented by Pierre-Marie Dupuy concerns not only states, but all those involved in environmental law, who may be guilty of environmental damage[60] . The obligation to repair damage caused is an important sanction in civil law. Environmental law, while borrowing this institution from civil law, adds its own borrowings in order to take proper account of the specific nature of environmental damage.

The enactment of standards and the detection of their violation require the existence of appropriate bodies to punish such violations.

In what follows, we shall briefly examine these dispute-settlement bodies in the more specific environmental field of air pollution.

§ 2 The institutional mechanism

The increasing dangers threatening the environment and the recognized need to protect it in recent decades have led States to set up a range of institutions designed to promote the principles and rules of environmental law.

At international level, there has been a proliferation of organizations that intervene directly or indirectly to ensure the sustainability of ecosystems. At the regional level in Africa, for example, they are supported in their missions by regional organizations which participate in their own way in environmental protection activities .[61]

To this end, these institutions, both universal (2.1) and regional (2.2), deserve to be presented.

2.1. *Universal institutions*

It should be noted that several bodies within the UN system are involved in

[59] Pierre-Marie Dupuy, op.cit.

[60] Aser NZOVU LUVUJI, *les techniques juridiques de la prévention de la pollution de l'eau*, éditions universitaires européennes, 2018, P. 132

[61] Emmanuel D. Kam Yogo, op.cit. P. 153

environmental protection at the universal level. This is true of the Security Council, the General Assembly and the International Court of Justice, which are the organization's main decision-making bodies on environmental issues.

The initiatives of other bodies, such as the Economic and Social Council and the General Secretariat, can only have legal or political effects if they are validated by the General Assembly or the Security Council.

It is also important to point out that only the jurisdictional institution will receive our particular attention in the treatment of this brief.

It is important to note that there are no specialized jurisdictions on a universal level to sanction environmental violations alone.

It is up to the existing jurisdictional bodies to deal with such disputes, namely the International Court of Justice (ICJ) and its Special Chamber, and the Arbitral Tribunal.

- ***The International Court of Justice and its special chamber on environmental matters***

The International Court of Justice is the principal judicial organ of the United Nations. Its mission is to settle disputes in accordance with international law, and to give advisory opinions. Following the proposals made at RIO in 1992 and the evolution of ideas concerning the place and role of the International Court of Justice in the settlement of disputes, in accordance with the provisions of Article 26 of its Statute, a special chamber was created within the Court in 1993 to deal with environmental issues.

In accordance with article 36 of the Statute, the Court's jurisdiction extends to all cases submitted to it by the parties to the dispute, as well as to all cases specially provided for in the Charter of the United Nations or in treaties or conventions in force.

Thus, the parties may also submit to the Court all legal disputes concerning the interpretation of a treaty, any point of international law, the reality of any fact which, if established, would constitute a breach of an international obligation, or the nature or extent of reparation due for the breach of an international obligation .[62]

Article 38 of the ICJ Statute clarifies this jurisdiction, stating that the Court, whose task is to settle disputes submitted to it in accordance with international law, shall apply international conventions, whether general or special, establishing rules

[62] Coffi Dieudonné ASSOUVI, *l'influence du droit international des changements climatiques sur le droit de l'environnement de l'union européenne*, Thesis, University of Limoges, 2018, P.467

expressly recognized by the States in dispute; international custom as evidence of a general practice accepted as law; the general principles of law recognized by civilized nations, judicial decisions and the doctrine of the most qualified publicists of the various nations as an auxiliary means of determining the rules of law.

Consequently, the Court can only hear a dispute if the States concerned have accepted its jurisdiction. No State can therefore be a party to a case before it (the Court) unless it has consented in one way or another . [63]

Under Article 34, paragraph 1 of the ICJ Statute, only States are entitled to appear before the Court. International organizations, public bodies and private individuals are consequently not entitled to initiate proceedings before the ICJ.

Through its jurisprudence, the ICJ has had occasion to rule on disputes with a significant environmental dimension. Such is the case of the aerial spraying of herbicides between Ecuador and Colombia, a case which was nevertheless removed from the Court's docket on September 13, 2013 at the request of the plaintiff. In its judgment of April 09, 1949 on the Carfou Strait case, the ICJ affirmed that "no State may use its territory for acts contrary to the rights of other States".

This position of the Court may well inspire the fight against transboundary pollution. Moreover, the specialized chamber on environmental issues has never been seized, and the ICJ decided in 2006 not to renew this body . [64]

- The arbitral tribunal

The arbitral settlement of disputes is instituted by various legal instruments, notably the Bamako Convention of January 30, 1991 on the Ban of the Import into Africa of Wastes and on the Control of Transboundary Movements and Management of Hazardous Wastes Generated in Africa, Article 5, point 2 of Annex V to this Convention.

At the end of our research, we noted the arbitration award in the Trail smelter case of March 11, 1941, made in the context of the settlement of disputes relating to the international law of air pollution. In any case, the arbitral tribunal makes its award in accordance with international law.

[63] See Article 36 § 5 of the ICJ Statute.

[64] Sandrine MALJEAN-DU BOIS, (dir), le droit de l'environnement comme exemple de la mondialisation des concepts juridiques : places et rôle des juridictions internationales et constitutionnelles, quoted by Coffi Dieudonné ASSOUVI, op.cit, P.469

2.2. *Regional institutions*

As a reminder, our study will focus solely on jurisdictional institutions. In particular, we will be looking at the European and African regional systems for combating air pollution.

Indeed, the jurisdictional mechanism for repressing air pollution at European regional level can be summed up essentially in the Court of Justice of the European Union (CJEU).

Its role is to ensure that European Union (EU) legislation is interpreted in the same way in all EU countries, and that EU countries and institutions comply with European legislation. Accordingly, it interprets European legislation to ensure uniform application in all EU countries, and rules on legal disputes between member governments and EU institutions.

In certain circumstances, individuals, companies or organizations may also bring a case against an EU institution if they feel their rights have been infringed.

With its mission of ensuring the correct application of EU legislation (action for failure to fulfil obligations), this procedure is applied when a member state fails to comply with EU legislation. It can be initiated by the European Commission or another member state.

If the infringement is found to have been committed, the country in question must put an end to it immediately, failing which it risks being the subject of a second appeal and the payment of a fine.

Through its case law, the European Court of Justice has given concrete expression to this mission to combat air pollution. On February 3, 2021, in its ruling C-637/18 Commission C. , the Court of Justice of the European Union found that Hungary had infringed Directive 2008/50 on air quality. Hungary that the latter (*Hungary)* had infringed Directive 2008/50 on air quality. This infringement involved exceeding the values set for PM_{10}micro-particles. It is worth pointing out that the Court has previously ruled against states in this area. These include Poland, Bulgaria, Romania and Italy.

The Court thus recalled that exceeding the limit value set for PM_{10}particles is sufficient to establish a breach of the first subparagraph of Article 13(1) and Annex XI of the Directive. Article 13, paragraph 1, subparagraph 1 of the above-mentioned directive requires Member States to ensure that levels of PM_{10}particles in the air do not exceed the limits set out in Annex XI to the directive.

In this judgment, the Court concluded that Hungary had failed to fulfil its obligations with regard to both the exceedance of the PM_{10}limit value in the areas concerned and its failure to ensure that the period of exceedance was as short as possible by drawing up an air quality plan.

This ruling is part of a wider context of air pollution control. It should be noted that infringement proceedings have been initiated against several other member states. The Commission C. Hungary judgment therefore contributes to achieving the objectives set out in the European Commission's communication and should ultimately lead to a cleaner environment in the European Union . [65]

The CJEU recently handed down its judgment on April 28, 2022 in case C-286/21, following an action brought on March 4, 2021 by the European Commission, as claimant, against the French Republic, as defendant, for failure to fulfil obligations under Article 258 TFEU.

The first claim alleges a systemic and persistent infringement of the combined provisions of Article 13(1) and Annex XI of Directive 2008/5; the second claim alleges an infringement of Article 23(1) of Directive 2008/50, read in conjunction with Annex XV thereto.

In examining the case, the Court (Tenth Chamber) declared and ruled: French Republic, by failing to ensure that the daily limit value applicable to concentrations of microparticles (PM_{10}) is not exceeded systematically and persistently since from January 1·2005 to 2019 inclusive, in the Paris conurbation and quality zone [...] by failing to ensure that air quality plans provide for appropriate measures to ensure that the period during which that limit value is exceeded is as short as possible, has failed, in both zones, since June 11, 2010, to fulfil its obligations under the second subparagraph of Article 23(1) of Directive 2008/50, read in conjunction with Annex XV thereto.

The French Republic was ordered to pay the costs.

Examination of the jurisdictional mechanism at the European regional level leads us to that of the African regional level.

At the African regional level, it should be noted that the African continent has developed a considerable legal arsenal in environmental matters. In addition to regional conventions, African states are signatories to most international texts relating

---

[65] Elisabeth Ruiz Cairo, *Effets du non-respect de la directive sur la qualité de l'air par les Etats membres*, CEJE news no. 4/2021, available at www.ceje.ch

to the right to the environment, in the wake of Article 24 of the African Charter on Human and Peoples' Rights of June 27 1981, adopted in Nairobi.

The African Court on Human and Peoples' Rights is the only continental jurisdiction currently operating in Africa. Article 3 of the Ouagadougou Protocol states that the "*Court shall have jurisdiction to hear all cases and disputes referred to it concerning the interpretation and application of the Charter*"[66] .

Under the terms of article 5-1 of the Ouagadougou Protocol, the following are entitled to bring cases before the Court: the Commission; the State party which has referred the case to the Commission; the State party against which a complaint has been lodged; the State party whose national is the victim of a human rights violation; and African international organizations. In addition, non-state actors have three main avenues of access to the African Court on Human and Peoples' Rights, to varying degrees: contentious appeals, amicus curiae and petitions.

There are two types of contentious appeal: direct and indirect. Direct referrals are based on article 5-3 of the Ouagadougou Protocol, which states that "the Court may allow individuals and non-governmental organizations (NGOs) having observer status with the Commission to submit petitions directly to it in accordance with article 34-6 of the Protocol".

Indirect referral to the Court is made via the Commission. Individuals or NGOs with observer status with the Commission can bring to the Commission's attention cases of human rights violations by a State.

Amicus curiae are provided for in article 70 of the Court's rules of procedure, which states: "All States parties may submit written observations on the points raised in the application. Any other interested entity may be authorized by the Court to do likewise".

Our study revealed that no case law has yet been developed by the African Court on Human and Peoples' Rights (CAFDHP) on the environment in general, and on air pollution specifically. It's hard to understand why this is the case in Africa, where the deterioration in air quality is enormous. This is often due to a lack of pollution detection equipment.

Nevertheless, the Commission, which has powers similar to those of the Court (see the provisions of Article 2 of the Ouagadougou Protocol), with the difference that

[66] See Revue Africaine de droit de l'environnement, la protection de l'environnement par les juridictions africaine : avancées nationales et régionales, N° 05. 2020, P.19

its decisions are not binding, has handed down two decisions relating to the environment. The first, concerning the SERAC case, found the Nigerian government guilty of violating articles
24 (right to the environment) and 16 (right to health) of the Charter, due to the environmental degradation inflicted on the Ogoni people as a result of oil exploitation carried out without prior environmental and social impact assessment and without prior consultation of this indigenous community.

In the second case, Endorois v. Kenya[67] , the Commission condemned the Kenyan government for having, by creating a nature reserve around Lake Bogoria, deprived the Endoris community of their ancestral lands, thereby damaging their pastoral and cultural activities.

The conviction was based on articles 21 and 22 of the charter, which deal respectively with the free disposal of resources and development.

A few decisions relating to the environment can nevertheless be found within African sub-regional jurisprudence, including the ECOWAS (Economic Community of Central African States) SERAP case, which is rooted in a petition of July 23, 2009 by which the socio-economic NGO Rights and Accountability project (SERAP) brought proceedings against Nigeria before the Abidjan Court, the Attorney General of Nigeria, the oil companies Nigeria National petroleum, shell petroleum development company, ELF petroleum Nigeria Ltd, AGIP Nigerian PLC, chevron Oil Nigeria PLC, Total Nigeria PLC and Exxan Mobil.

The applicant complained of the violation of the right to health, to quality of life, to a healthy environment and to economic and social development of the populations of the Niger Delta by the above-mentioned oil companies due to their uncontrolled exploitation of oil and subsequent pollution. Such is the case of Africa Network for Animal welfare (ANAW) vs the Attorney general of the united Republic of Tanzania (August 29, 2011).

Like the CAFDHP, an analysis of the case law of the UEMOA Court of Justice reveals a curious absence of decisions directly or indirectly relating to environmental matters. It is therefore imperative to examine the causes of this situation in the lines that follow.

---

[67] Center for Minority Rights Development (Kenya) and Minority Right (on behalf of Endoris welfare council) v. Kenya (2009), African Commission on Human and Peoples' Rights, n° 276/03, 49^{eme}session, 27^{eme}activity report.

An analysis of the normative and institutional (jurisdictional) framework for combating air pollution, as examined above, provides ample evidence of its limited effectiveness.

CHAPTER II. THE LIMITED EFFECTIVENESS OF AIR POLLUTION CONTROL MECHANISMS IN DIE

Air pollution control mechanisms at both universal and regional levels have already been described in the previous chapter. These mechanisms could only be foreseen with the aim of effectively preventing air pollution. For this goal to be achieved, it is certainly true that these mechanisms must be effective and guarantee their applicability.

The study carried out reveals that the effectiveness of these air pollution control mechanisms is low, and it is appropriate first to illustrate this (section 1), before presenting the factors that make them weak in terms of effectiveness (section 2).

Section 1: Illustration of low effectiveness

For the purposes of this study, the low effectiveness of air pollution control mechanisms will be illustrated at both universal (§1) and regional (§2) levels. These mechanisms are made up of legal instruments and jurisdictional institutions.

§.1. *On a universal scale*

As already emphasized in relation to Michel PRIEUR's indicators, the effectiveness of the law implies that the rule exists, that it is legally applicable, that it is respected, applied and controlled, and that it is eventually sanctioned by the administration and the courts.

From a normative point of view, it has to be said that there is no universal international environmental convention. However, we have noted a number of texts that deal specifically with air quality issues (especially at the European regional level), and others that do not deal with them specifically, but at least allude to pollution in general.

Moreover, despite the considerable existence of legal instruments, many of them lack binding force.

From the point of view of jurisdictional mechanisms, there is an almost total absence of special environmental jurisdictions. The only ICJ that can rule on the matter has not issued a single decision relating to air pollution.

The only such decision was handed down by the Arbitral Tribunal in the trail smelter case.

This lack of effectiveness on a universal scale is further evidenced by the poor applicability of existing legal instruments by the international jurisdiction (ICJ), as evidenced by the absence of decisions on the subject and the inadequacy of decisions taken by arbitral tribunals.

§.2. At regional level

The question of the low effectiveness of air pollution enforcement mechanisms at regional level is moderated at European level, unlike at African level.

Referring to the legal indicators proposed by Mr. Prieur and the analysis above, it follows that, from both the normative and institutional standpoints, specific rules for combating air pollution have been established at the European regional level. This is also the case with the various judicial decisions handed down by the CJEU in abundance to punish deviant behavior in relation to air pollution.

The most recent of these rulings was against France, not to mention all the case law handed down by the Court of Justice of the European Union since its creation.

On the other hand, the situation appears to be the opposite at the African regional level, where no jurisprudence or, better still, no jurisdictional decision has been noted in relation to air pollution in the jurisprudential arsenal of the African Court of Human and Peoples' Rights, which is the only continental jurisdiction currently operating in Africa.

And yet, from a normative point of view, there is a whole range of legal instruments adopted at African regional level relating to the preservation of the environment, including the first regional legal instrument for the protection of human rights to formally enshrine the right to a healthy environment, the African Charter on Human and Peoples' Rights. The same observation applies to the African sub-region.

Now that the manifestations of weak effectiveness have been identified, it is necessary to determine the factors that render this effectiveness weak.

Section 2. The endogenous and exogenous factors behind the low effectiveness of mechanisms for repressing air pollution in EIS.

Generally speaking, environmental law is poorly implemented[68]. And in the context of our study, it is necessary to stress that several factors are at the root of this

[68] Yacouba Savadogo, *la protection communautaire de l'environnement dans le cadre de l'UEMOA : enjeux, portée et perspectives*, thesis, université de limoges, 2019, P.369

weak effectiveness of air pollution repression mechanisms, which consequently create numerous negative effects on the environmental, State, legal and health levels.

These factors are both endogenous (§1) and exogenous (§2).

§1 Endogenous factors

The endogenous factors that make the repression of air pollution ineffective can be presented from both the normative and jurisdictional standpoints. They are said to be endogenous, because they (factors) lie within the norm and the jurisdictional institution.

Indeed, from a normative point of view, it has to be said that the various legal instruments for combating air pollution are not dissuasive, in that they make almost no provision for sanctions against States or perpetrators who violate their obligations to preserve and conserve the environment in general, and to combat air pollution in particular.

The various existing declarations of environmental rights, which are purely symbolic, have no legal scope and can rarely be invoked directly before the courts .[69]

The majority of these instruments focus on the amicable settlement or arbitration of any dispute between the parties to the said instruments, prior to referral to the competent international jurisdiction, but they are silent on the procedure to be followed and the various stages to be completed.

In our view, the absence of sanctions in these instruments, and the lack of mechanisms for resolving disputes amicably or through arbitration, make the fight against air pollution rather ineffective.

Indeed, these methods of resolving disputes have the not inconsiderable consequence of making little use of the courts.

The majority of environmental offences, even the most serious, are resolved through settlements, thus limiting recourse to the courts.

And yet, as we all know, the role of the judge is to apply the sanctions provided for by law, by pronouncing sentences and/or imposing reparations or fines on any offender; thus enabling the legal norm to play its dissuasive role.

Added to this list of endogenous factors is the absence of effective bodies to monitor and control its implementation, especially at the African regional level.

[69] Rapport du club des juristes, op.cit. P.45

From a jurisdictional point of view, it must first be noted that few international environmental conventions provide for real sanction mechanisms. They prefer a cooperative approach to a punitive one.

Enforcement often takes the form of so-called non-compliance procedures, entrusted to simple committees with no decision-making powers, which result not in condemnation by a judicial body but in assistance for countries failing to meet their commitments.

In addition, as the report by the Club des Juristes[70] reveals, when states know they are at risk of being sanctioned, they can often denounce an international agreement at any time. For example, under the threat of sanctions, Canada, which had far exceeded its targets (emissions up 28% instead of down 6%), unilaterally withdrew from the Kyoto Protocol in December 2011. The international legal order is thus marked by the primacy of consent.

Nonetheless, a number of court rulings on air pollution have been noted in the course of this report, even if they are not very dissuasive, since an order to pay costs alone, for example, would do little to change the deviant behavior of those responsible for pollution. The severity of the penalties imposed by the judge can act as a deterrent and help to ensure the effectiveness of air pollution control mechanisms.

§.2. Exogenous factors

The low effectiveness of air pollution enforcement mechanisms is also due to certain exogenous factors, which are not necessarily linked to legal rules or to the nature of the decisions handed down by the courts, but which render the norm weakly applied or almost inapplicable by the courts.

When a legal action is brought, the judge applies the standard, which calls on the latter to hand down a judicial decision. However, despite the existence of certain established standards, the parties prefer not to go to court.

Such is the case of Côte d'Ivoire, which, despite the existence of legal instruments on the subject, in particular the 1991 Bamako Convention on the Ban of the Import into Africa and the Control of the Movement of Hazardous Wastes within Africa, to which it (Côte d'Ivoire) is an integral member following its ratification on

---

[70] Idem, P.30

July 13, 1994, the Ivorian authorities dropped the legal proceedings following a financial agreement of 152.5 million Euros (100 billion FCFA) paid by Trafigura to the Ivorian State to compensate the victims of pollution of all kinds due to highly toxic waste of a total volume of 528 m3, composed of caustic soda and sulfur products dumped in open public dumps and in various places in the city of Abidjan.

It should also be noted that the proliferation of environmental protection standards contrasts with the fact that they are poorly promoted among the general public. The population is largely unaware of the subjective rights it enjoys, even though it is the main holder of these rights.

Another factor is the technical nature of environmental law, the mastery of which remains the monopoly of professionals (insiders) who have acquired appropriate training.

Added to this is the fact that some judges have a poor grasp of environmental law. In fact, environmental law is largely absent from the standard training given to some judges, especially at regional level in Africa, which reflects their reluctance to deal with environmental disputes.

The inability of certain players to take legal action (NGOs, for example) in certain countries, or even before the ICJ, may be one of the exogenous factors behind the low effectiveness of air pollution enforcement mechanisms. Indeed, we are well aware of the role and influence of NGOs in environmental protection;

All the above elements of analysis allow us to conclude on the current state of air pollution control mechanisms. The conclusion is clear. These mechanisms have enormous weaknesses which undermine even the effectiveness of their action.

To this end, it is appropriate to present the relevance of this assessment in the analysis of the second part.

PART TWO: ASSESSING THE EFFICIENCY OF AIR POLLUTION CONTROL MECHANISMS IN INTERNATIONAL ENVIRONMENTAL LAW ENVIRONMENTAL LAW

The study of air pollution repression mechanisms in IEL has just been outlined in the first part. To this end, these mechanisms could only be envisaged with the aim of effectively and efficiently preventing air pollution. And yet, in order to achieve this goal, these mechanisms must be effective and efficient, and must be enforceable.

Thus, the weakness or failure of these mechanisms can undoubtedly have negative effects or impacts on the effectiveness of repressive action (chapter 1). For example, when a legal instrument lacks dissuasive measures, it will be difficult for the judicial institution to take effective action in the field by issuing dissuasive decisions.

The relevance of the low effectiveness of air pollution repression mechanisms observed above will be presented by means of an evaluation of the effectiveness and efficiency of the said mechanisms.

It should also be noted that the evaluation of legal mechanisms can be based on several criteria. Legal doctrine relating to the quality of positive law in certain Western countries, organizes various criteria for critical assessments of the quality of law. These criteria can be divided into six groups, including objectivity, effectiveness, efficiency, legitimacy, efficacy and operationality . [71]

It is undoubtedly difficult, not to say perilous, to assess the effectiveness of environmental law, especially in the presence of a profusion of legal rules applicable to fields as varied as the environment, and in the absence of consensual criteria for evaluating effectiveness. However, like Charles Visscher, we can consider that a legal norm is effective or ineffective depending on whether or not it proves "capable of determining the desired behaviour in those concerned".

In other words, it is the receptiveness of the legal norm to its addressee that determines its effectiveness. In the specific field of the environment, this criterion of the norm's receptiveness may prove highly relevant, insofar as the legislator's objective is, after all, to obtain a change in citizens' behaviour towards the environment.

However, however interesting it may be, the criterion of receptiveness to environmental norms is not in itself sufficient to assess the effectiveness of environmental law. Hence Sandrine Maljean-Dubois' analysis of the implementation of international environmental law, which identifies five indicators of the effectiveness of international environmental law. In her view, an IEL can be deemed effective if it:

[71] AMOS Maurice, *critères d'évaluation critique de la qualité d'une loi ou d'un instrument équivalent*, available at: https://www.village-justice.com/articles/critères-evaluation-critique-qualite-une-loi-instrument- equivalent 27150.html, [accessed 03 July 2022]

- ✓ Ensures environmental protection ;
- ✓ Leads to compliance with the rules and standards laid down;
- ✓ Leads to the desired change in human behavior;
- ✓ Is transposed to different levels (regional, national, local) through the adoption of laws, regulations and the conduct of certain administrative activities;
- ✓ Has an impact through its mere existence, independently of the adoption of specific measures.

Without going into the details of the various criteria, it should be noted that the legitimacy criterion for evaluating legal instruments is based on applicability, the guarantee of justice, general interest and relevance. These parameters make it possible to evaluate a legal instrument in terms of its applicability.

The applicability of a legal instrument, or rather its legitimate applicability or legitimate application, makes it possible to assess the usefulness and basis of its application. For public actors (authorities), it assesses their ability to assert their authority, to balance established rules, to guarantee the principles of equality, legality and balance between rules and freedoms, and to make rational choices . [72]

It also assesses the ability of the authorities to deal with problems in the field, and to secure the tacit validation of their actions, the tacit and consensual agreement or overall assent of the governed.

According to Michel Coutou, legitimate application also takes into account rationality in terms of means, objectives, consequences and value, as well as law that is innovative, calculable, far-sighted, coherent, complete, based on logical qualities and precisely predictable[73] . The guarantee of justice, for its part, consists in knowing in what way the law or legal instrument makes it possible to delegitimize or not legitimize state oppression, as Karl Marx informs us[74] The criterion of legitimacy in the guarantee of justice also applies to the general interest. This involves verifying, in particular, the interest of this instrument for the collectivity it concerns in a general way; the elements by which it makes it possible to maintain or guarantee public order and satisfy collective needs and the unfavorable causes of particularism, nepotism,

[72] John Rawls, *Theory of Justice*, Threshold, Paris, 1997, P.46
[73] Michel Coutou, *Max Weber et les rationalités du droit*, LGDJ, Paris, 1995, P.87
[74] Quoted by AMOS Maurice, op.cit.

favoritism, partiality, inequalities or social imbalances, illicit enrichment, oppression of the governed, disinterest in the collectivity, particular interests prejudicial to the general interest . [75]

Efficiency also assesses the objective usefulness, importance or interest of the effects sought or achieved.

The low effectiveness of air pollution control mechanisms in EIS, as noted above, may reflect the environmental, state, legal and health relevance of their effects. So, to improve this situation of effectiveness in order to expect efficient results, some recommendations in terms of future prospects prove useful (chapter II).

[75] Michel De Villiers and Thibaut De Berranger (dir), Droit public général : institutions politiques, administratives et européennes, droit administratif, finances publiques et droit fiscal, Lexis Nexis, Paris, 2015, quoted by Aser NZOVU LUVUJI, Thèse de doctorat, op.cit., P.177

CHAPTER I : INEFFECTIVENESS OF AIR POLLUTION REPRESSION MECHANISMS IN DIE

The air pollution control mechanisms we have examined have a number of weaknesses which undermine their effectiveness in controlling air pollution. The ineffectiveness of these mechanisms (normative and institutional) will be developed in this chapter (section 1).

The effectiveness of the importance of the mechanisms in an action to be taken is essential. Comparing the notion of effectiveness with that of the efficacy of the rule of law, Yann Leroy notes that, while the evaluation of efficacy is concerned only with desired effects, the broader assessment of efficacy is also concerned with unintended effects .[76]

In Maud Gautier's view, effectiveness is a way of assessing the consequences of legal norms and their suitability for the ends they aim to achieve[77] . Thus, the above review of air pollution control mechanisms reveals a gloomy picture, peppered with a number of weaknesses that affect their effectiveness. Hence, the impact of this ineffectiveness will be addressed (section 2), before recommending some future prospects, as mentioned above.

SECTION 1: NORMATIVE AND INSTITUTIONAL INEFFICIENCY

The analysis will focus on "normative" legal instruments (§1) on the one hand, and on "jurisdictional" institutional mechanisms (§2) on the other.

§.1 "Normative" legal instruments

Almost all the legal instruments used to combat air pollution have a number of weaknesses that make them ineffective in the fight against air pollution. However relevant they may be, legal rules do not in themselves produce the expected effects.

More often than not, their effectiveness depends on the means of control implemented by the public authorities to ensure compliance. Environmental protection rules are no exception to this rule . [78]

---

[76] Yann Leroy, op.cit. consulted on July 04, 2022

[77] Maud Gautier, *Effectivité, efficience et efficacité...Le nouvel essor du concept de performance contractuelle*, quoted by Aser NZOVU LUVUJI, Thèse de doctorat, op.cit. P. 218

[78] Laurent Granier, (coord.), Aspects contemporains du droit de l'environnement en Afrique de l'ouest et centrale. IUCN, Gland, Switzerland. Xvi, 2008, P.18

Indeed, the control of standards is institutionalized. Firstly, procedures are institutionalized; collectivized, control loses its traditional reciprocal character. It is thus entrusted to the ad hoc bodies created by the various environmental protection conventions, exercised by the Conferences of the Parties, committees and secretariats which perform this task.

This is the case of the Bamako Convention, by way of illustration, which refers the control of the standard to a national body designated for this purpose by the parties (it should be remembered that this aspect of the control of the standard was mentioned in the previous lines). Environmental protection rules suffer from a cruel lack of control. The structures charged with carrying out this control are not exercising the powers accorded to them by law, and their effectiveness is therefore affected.

Beyond this aspect of control, it should be noted that the majority of environmental protection texts adopted at international (universal) or regional level do not define the offences or even the penalties that polluters may incur.

The effectiveness of a rule of law in a legal arsenal largely depends on its status or the way in which it is formulated. It may be stated in general terms, as a principle, or in precise detail. When stated in general terms, it even lacks normative consistency, requiring implementation by other legal instruments to bring out its normative consistency and make it suitable for application in a given case.

And yet, as demonstrated above, the various legal instruments that govern the environment in general, and air in particular, at the universal level have a number of weaknesses, leaving the door open to parties to take measures at the domestic level to establish certain behaviours as infringements, as well as the means of resolving them. This decision-making process is normally accompanied by policies, plans and strategies for implementing the rule. In our view, this is a sign of the unfinished nature of the normative process at international level.

The majority of the existing body of law shows a major weakness. The various existing declarations of environmental rights, which are purely symbolic, have no legal scope and can rarely be invoked directly before the courts.

§.2. Jurisdictional aspects

It is important, even judicious, to note that this normative ineffectiveness often has unfortunate repercussions for the courts, which are called upon to implement the texts thus enacted with a view to protecting the environment in general, and the air in particular, by imposing sanctions on those responsible for violating the said texts.

Indeed, sanctions are the key to the effectiveness of any normative mechanism. It can also be perceived as a penalty or repressive measure, the natural consequence of an act in connection with a prohibition, an injunction or a certain way of acting.

Thus, some authors consider sanctions [...] to be the surest means of ensuring compliance with the rule of law and, as a consequence of this reasoning, the best guarantee of its effectiveness, [or] the essential condition of its effectiveness[79] . The importance of sanctions led Hans Kelsen to equate the effectiveness of the rule of law with its application.

For him, a norm is effective [...] when it is applied in concrete cases by the organs of the judicial order, by the Courts, i.e. when the sanction is ordered and executed [...] . [80]

Curiously, the institutional (judicial) mechanism suffers from a decision-making deficiency. Rarely seized of environmental issues, judicial bodies do not often have the opportunity to rule on such matters. And yet, there is no lack of environmentally damaging behaviour that could be punished. In fact, some classified establishments are the source of serious environmental damage and air pollution, yet no legal proceedings are taken against them.

In the fight against air pollution, for example, the administrative authorities hardly punish any of the perpetrators of pollution, and are content to bribe them while encouraging such deterioration in air quality. Numerous classified establishments are set up and operate on the bangs of regulations relating to classified, unhealthy and

---

[79] According to Guillaume Drago, effectiveness is the concrete, practical realization of the rule of law, its execution and application by those to whom it is addressed: see Id, "l'effectivité des sanctions de la violation des droits fondamentaux dans les pays de la communauté francophone", in AUPELF, colloque international, Port-Louis, 29-30 Sept et 1er oct. 1993, AUPELF-UREF, 1994, P. 535 quoted by Yann Leroy, op.cit. and Aser NZOVU LUVUJI, Thèse de doctorat, op.cit., P. 224.

[80] Idem

inconvenient establishments, without being subject to any legal proceedings . [81]

International environmental law is characterized by its lack of effectiveness and efficiency, in that it often seems incapable of producing the effects it has been assigned or the behaviour it would like to encourage (see Sandrine Maljean-Dubois' indicators). In fact, it suffers not only from the inadequacy of the means for monitoring its application, as mentioned above, but also from the weakness of the penalties for non-compliance with its standards.

The few decisions pinpointed in this brief are not dissuasive in nature, and are therefore ineffective in producing the desired effects. And yet, a careful examination of the various national legislations of the various countries shows that air pollution is punished with great rigor. For example, article 82 of law no. 96/12 of August 5, 1996, the framework law on environmental management in Cameroon, states that :

Is punishable by a fine of one million (1,000,000) to five million (5,000,000) FCFA and imprisonment of six (6) months to one (1) year or one of these penalties only, any person who pollutes, degrades [...] alters the quality of the air [...], in violation of the provisions of this law.

Under Congolese law (D.R. Congo), penalties for air pollution range from six months to three years' penal servitude and a fine of between five million and fifty million Congolese francs, in accordance with article 79 of law no. 11/009 of July 09, 2011 on the fundamental principles of environmental protection, which stipulates that:

Any person who alters the quality of the air in violation of the provisions of the present law and its enforcement measures shall be punished by a penal servitude of six months to three years and a fine of five million to fifty million Congolese francs, or by one of these penalties only. It is curious to note, however, that these enforcement measures have unfortunately never been taken in the air pollution sector, and these sanctions suffer from their application.

Air quality is the result of a whole range of public policies, whether related to transport organization, urban planning, agricultural policy or public health. The many instruments implemented for emitting sectors, which have been stratified over time and are not all specific to air quality policy, need to be better articulated, as the

---

[81] Club des juristes report, op.cit. p. 20

consequences can be very unfortunate.

Hence the importance of analyzing the consequences of the ineffectiveness of these mechanisms in the lines that follow.

Section 2: IMPACT OF THE INEFFECTIVENESS OF REPRESSION MECHANISMS OF AIR POLLUTION IN DIE

The impact of the ineffectiveness of these mechanisms can have far-reaching consequences, both in environmental and state terms (§1), and in legal and health terms (§2).

§.1. Consequences for the environment and the state

Since the mechanisms put in place by the EIS to combat air pollution are not very effective, and are therefore inefficient, the repercussions can only be immense, both environmentally (1.1) and in terms of the state (1.2). We will outline some of these consequences in the development that follows.

1.1. Environmental impact

At the outset, it's important to note that the environmental issue highlights the growing interdependence of more than just the components of the earth's ecosystem. It will be recalled that at the Earth Summit in 1992, States recognized that the Earth, the home of humanity, constitutes a whole marked by interdependence. The environmental issue also highlights the interdependencies between States and between States and private economic players. Environmental governance calls for a number of recompositions, including the reorganization of normative processes, in order to make the various players more accountable. And this is no simple matter . [82]

The environment is the source of all life on earth, enabling us to feed ourselves. It is the source not only of food and drinking water, but also of clean air, oxygen and so on.

The ineffectiveness of air pollution control mechanisms is having a negative impact on the environment. Polluted air floating on the Earth's surface can be carried long distances by the wind or rain, affecting many other sectors or components of the environment, including water, soil and the ecosystem as a whole. In other words, air

[82] Lire dans ce sens, Actes du séminaire organisé par la plateforme RSE (responsabilité sociale des entreprises) sous le thème, *le rôle du droit dans la protection de l'environnement*, septembre 2018, sous la coordination de Kathia MARTIN - CHENUT, P. 9

pollution is a phenomenon with multiple negative impacts.

Such is the case with the accumulation of gases in the atmosphere, which generates environmental facts with unfortunate consequences, such as the depletion of the ozone layer, acid rain, global warming, the greenhouse effect and many other facts with similar consequences.

It follows that this pollution also has consequences for the evolution of plants in relation to photosynthesis and air purification.

Indeed, from a climatic point of view - and this is nothing new - emissions of numerous pollutants into the air (ozone, carbon soot, carbon dioxide, particles...) are toxic and harmful both to health (which we shall discuss below) and to the environment. To understand these interactions, let's take a closer look at two of them: soot carbon (also known as black carbon) and carbon dioxide (CO2), both of which contribute to the greenhouse effect.

Sooty carbon, a carbon compound whose black color absorbs light radiation, can influence the radioactive balance by warming the atmosphere. It is part of the PM2,5 fine particulate matter (diameter less than 2.5µm) and also comes from combustion engines (mainly diesel), wood and coal combustion, power plants, the use of heavy fuel oil or coal, the combustion of agricultural waste as well as forest and vegetation fires.

A 2013 American study highlights the extreme responsibility of soot carbon in global warming, making it the 2ndndfactor after CO2. Sooty carbon, present in the air as an aerosol (mixed with other particles), has a lifetime in the atmosphere of a few days to a few weeks at most; by comparison, CO2 has a lifetime of 100 years. So, for the same emissions, soot carbon causes a short-lived heat peak, whereas CO2 warms the atmosphere for a long time . [83]

It would be wrong not to consider CO2 as an air pollutant, given its natural presence in the atmosphere and its role in the cycle of life. Under human influence, CO2 levels in the atmosphere have been rising steadily for millions of years. A sharp rise of 30% has been observed over the last two centuries. While the effects of CO2 on human health are slight when it is present in "natural" quantities in the atmosphere, when its concentration rises sharply, it becomes an environmental

[83] Research carried out by 31 scientists and published in the online version of the American journal Geophysical Research-atmospheres.

pollutant in the strict sense of the term . [84]

According to Daniel JACOBS, Professor of Atmospheric Chemistry at Harvard University, "warming induces more stagnation and accumulation of polluted air, the reactions that make ozone occur more rapidly, and nitrous oxide (one of ozone's precursors) has a longer life at warmer temperatures "[85] . The quality of the air we breathe depends on the lifestyle choices we make every day.

Air pollution also has an impact on soil and water resources. Indeed, it can considerably deteriorate the quality of soil and water resources.

Starting with the effects on soil, for example, acid precipitation can alter the chemical composition of soil, which in turn can affect global growth and water quality in a number of ways.

As soil becomes more acidic, its ability to retain many essential nutrients, minerals and elements, such as calcium (Ca), magnesium (Mg) and potassium (K), diminishes. These are then transported or leached by the water flowing through the soil, making them less available to the organisms that live there[86] . We can also note that many human activities can have deleterious effects on our seas, rivers, lakes and water tables.

Water quality is influenced by direct discharges, such as those from a factory or wastewater treatment plant: this is point-source pollution.

It is also influenced by pollution from various sources, such as fertilizers and pesticides used in agricultural activities, and pollutants released into the air by industry, which then fall back to the ground and the sea: this is known as diffuse pollution . [87]

The consequences can also be felt in vegetation. Plants are directly or indirectly damaged by various atmospheric pollutants. Pollutants and problems of

---

[84] Note available at: https://www.teqoya.fr/rechauffement-climatique-pollution/

[85] Idem

[86] Available at: https://www.canada.ca/fr/environnement-changement- climatique/services/pollution-atmospherique/qualite-environnement-economie/ecosysteme/effet-sol- eau.html

[87] Note available at: https://www.eea.europa.eu/fr/help/questions-frequemment-posees/quelles- sont-les-principales-sources

particular concern include tropospheric ozone, a major component of smog, acid rain and sulfur dioxide (SO_2).

The effect of poor air quality on plants can be acute (rapid and considerable), chronic (long-term) or hidden. Often, the symptoms of air pollution are visually similar to the natural aging of leaves during autumn, but this pollution can cause these conditions to appear earlier than normal.

In general, plants grow less rapidly and may become more vulnerable to drought and cold. The exception may be nitrogen-deficient ecosystems, which may experience a period of increased growth when exposed to nitrogen oxides (NOx) and the resulting acid rain. It should be noted that acid precipitation can damage plants in a variety of ways. Increased soil acidity can reduce the amount of nutrients and essential elements that plants can absorb. Acidity can also prevent root systems from absorbing these same nutrients. Acid precipitation can also damage leaf and needle surfaces.

Animals, or wildlife, are not immune to the effects of air pollution.

Pollutants of concern include acid rain, heavy metals, persistent organic pollutants (POPs) and other toxic substances. Here it should be noted that air pollution can be detrimental to wildlife in two main ways:

- ✓ *It deteriorates the quality of t h e environment or habitat i n which animals live;*
- ✓ *It reduces the availability and quality of the food supply.*

Building on the effects of atmospheric pollution on habitat quality, animals live on and in the ground, as well as in water. They must also breathe air using lungs, gills or another form of gas exchange, such as passive diffusion through the surface of the skin. All these conditions influence an animal's vulnerability to the effects of atmospheric pollution.

The effects of air pollution on food supply and quality Many heavy metals, toxic substances, persistent organic pollutants (POPs) and other air pollutants are harmful to wildlife by entering the food chain and influencing food supply and quality.

Once consumed, many of these pollutants accumulate and are stored in animal tissues. When eaten by other animals in the trophic chain, these pollutants continue to accumulate and increase in concentration. These air pollutants can be toxic to animals by disrupting their endocrine function, damaging their organs, increasing their vulnerability to stress and disease, reducing their reproductive success and possibly causing their death .[88]

In view of the environmental impact of air pollution as outlined above, it is clearly admissible to assert that between air pollution and the ecosystem, there is a complex and vulnerable set of relationships. a complex and vulnerable set of relationships.

The term ecosystem underlines the fact that the living and inanimate elements of the environment, including humans, are all part of a highly interconnected and interdependent system of life. Ecosystems and the organisms within them are not static. They continually evolve and adapt to new environmental conditions and relationships. The survival of species depends on their ability to adapt to change.

However, pollutants disrupt the balance and energy flow of the ecosystem. They can poison organisms and cause rapid, harmful changes in the environment. These changes can stress certain species, making them more vulnerable to disease and seasonal conditions such as drought and cold, and reducing their ability to respond and survive. Different pollutants give rise to different environmental concerns. The effect of air pollution can also be felt differently by each species or individual within a species.

As a result of air pollution, an ecosystem can become quite different from the one we are familiar with or depend on. The potential consequences of these changes throughout the ecosystem remain of great concern . [89]

Now that the impact of the lack of effectiveness of air pollution control mechanisms on the environmental level has been fully developed, it is appropriate to present the impact on the state level in the second section, before presenting the

[88] See the data available at: https://www.canada.ca/fr/environnement-changement- climate/services/pollution-atmospherique/qualite-environnement-economie/ecosysteme/effet-sol- eau.html

[89] Idem

impact on the legal and health levels.

1.2. State impact

What about the State? Before going any further, we'd like to define the concept of the "*State*".

In Frank Baron's view, the State is both a historical reality, which explains the difficulty of defining it in a fully satisfactory manner.

On the other hand, the notion of the State belongs to the vocabulary of public law to designate a sovereign unit formed by populations living on a defined territory and recognized as a legal and political organization of international society . [90]

In his contributions to the general theory of the State (1921), the jurist Carré de Malberg defines the latter as a community of men, fixed on its own territory and possessing an organization from which the group envisaged in its relations with its members derives a supreme power of action, command and coercion. He underlines the dual meaning of the concept, where the state corresponds :

- ✓ On the one hand, to a territorially defined mode of social organization;
- ✓ on the other, to a set of institutions characterized by a monopoly on the rule of law and the use of public force.

It follows that the modern understanding of the notion of the State actually emerged during the Renaissance, when the divine foundation of social order was radically challenged. The model of the Greek city or the Roman empire fueled the criteria against the medieval system of power, still marked by the influence of the Church and the feudal division of sovereignty. Thus, the Florentine Nicolas Machiavelli (1469 - 1527) defined the State as the sovereign central power, and detached political action from any moral or religious considerations . [91]

Starting with the legal characteristics of the state, the main criterion defining the state is the exercise of sovereignty, which is an unconditional power from which all other powers derive. This means that, within the territory for which it is responsible, the State has the power to exercise its competences.

When this sovereignty is exercised by a single institutional unit, the State is

---

[90] Serge Braudo, *legal dictionary*, available online at: https://www.dictionnaire- juridique.com/definition/etat.php

[91] Vie publique, available at: https://www.vie-publique.fr/parole-dexpert/270243-qest-ce-que-letat

unitary. When it is shared between several states, themselves grouped within a single state unit, it is called a federal state.

The state also plays an essential role on the international stage, as it is responsible for defending its population and territory.

To this end, the state can enter into binding agreements with other states, while at the same time possessing armed force: it thus acts both as a subject of international law and as a power . [92]

Without wishing to dwell too long on the notion of the State, it is important now to return to the impact of the ineffectiveness of air pollution control mechanisms on this entity, the State.

Indeed, from the point of view of the principal actors, international environmental law remains the prerogative of the States[93] . Far be it from us to set aside the other players, who also play a vital role in environmental protection in general, including the I.O. (international organizations). Conventional standards, like others, must be followed by action; in the broadest sense of the term, they must be applied. However, they are not always applied, and their non-application occurs in a wide variety of circumstances and circumstances . [94]

The application of international norms can, to a certain extent, engage the responsibility of actors who have committed illicit or reprehensible acts. In the case under consideration, this would be the responsibility of the State. As far as the responsibility of the latter (the State) is concerned, we could go back a long way in our thinking.

Thus, responsibility in the generic sense of the term refers to the obligation to answer for, and assume responsibility for, the legal consequences of conduct. To this end, any internationally wrongful act by a State must engage its international responsibility. But because of the specific characteristics of the international community, made up of sovereign subjects, international responsibility has its own specific features.

In this respect, NADAUD notes that international responsibility is often understood strictly as the obligation incumbent, under international law, on the State to which an act or omission contrary to its international obligations is attributable, to

---

[92] Idem

[93] Jacqueline Maurand-Deviller, *le droit de l'environnement*, presses universitaires de France, 2015, PP.21 - 33

[94] Paul Reuter, *introduction au droit des traités*, graduate institute publications, Geneva, 1985, PP.145 - 183

provide reparation to the State which has been the victim thereof in itself or in the persons, property or environment of its nationals . [95]

On this basis, State responsibility is engaged at international level when conduct attributable to the State constitutes a breach of an international obligation of the latter before the International Court of Justice (ICJ), before which only States are entitled to appear, damage not being a necessary condition for this engagement . [96]

The understanding of State responsibility in the treatment of the present work should not focus on the internationally wrongful act, which, moreover, is proving to be in part unsuited to damage caused to the environment, but rather and above all on conduct attributable to the State causing damage as a result of polluting activities or any other activity having untoward and detrimental consequences for the environment.

The latter is understood in its general sense. This is because the exercise of certain activities by the State which, at the outset, do not conflict with international law, may be a cause of environmental degradation and may engage the State's responsibility in this respect.

On the basis of all these considerations, if legal instruments are ineffective and the sanction to be reserved for the State to engage its responsibility is not dissuasive (effective), this will result in the perpetuation of the prejudicial behaviour of the said State with regard to the environment; recidivism on its part by normalizing air pollution. Hence, it would be ideal if the common interest, in particular that of preserving a healthy, unpolluted environment where everyone can breathe clean air, were to take precedence over selfish interest.

§.2 Legal and health impact

According to Julien Bétaille, sanctions, or rather repression, raise the question of the very raison d'être of environmental standards[97] . Hence, the low effectiveness and inefficiency of air pollution repression mechanisms also have an impact on both the legal (2.1.) and health (2.2) fronts.

---

[95] Séverine NADAUD, *la responsabilité internationale en matière d'environnement*, course n°8, option 1, University of Limoges, "envidroit" digital campus, P.2

[96] Idem

[97] Julien Bétaille, *répression et effectivité de la norme environnementale*, in revue juridique de l'environnement, 2014/HSO1 Volume 39, article available online at: https://www.cair.info/revue-juridique-de-l- environnement-2014-HSO1-page-47.htm [accessed July 10, 2022]

2.1. On the legal front

It is worth noting that several other elements of the legal system contribute to effectiveness, such as the legitimacy of the norm, the quality of its elaboration, the confidence of those to whom the norm is addressed, and its interpretation, as well as its sanction. Consequently, repression, which is one of the legal conditions for the norm's effectiveness, comes into play[98]. However, the contribution of sanctions and repression to effectiveness can be clearly demonstrated, since their function in the legal system is to ensure compliance with the norm.

It follows that the function of sanctions within the legal order is thus to dissuade legal subjects from violating norms. The function of punishment, of repressive law, is thus to contribute to compliance with the norm and its effectiveness. In other words, punishment only fulfils its function within the legal system if it succeeds in dissuading violations of the norm.

For Jean Rivero, the fear of the gendarme and the judge is expected to be enough to keep those tempted to deviate from the law on the path to compliance[99]. More generally, sanctions have a preventive function. Its effective intervention dissuades future deviations from the norm. On a theoretical level, the mere existence of sanctions as secondary legal norms serves to prevent non-compliance with the norm.

Hans Kelsen explains that the ideal case of a legal norm's validity is realized if it does not come into force at all, because the representation of the sanction that would intervene in the event of an offence determines all subjects subject to the legal order not to commit this offence .[100]

Furthermore, a sanction that is too weak or non-existent has no dissuasive effect, and therefore cannot fulfil its function. The sanction must be sufficiently severe, and have a credible chance of convincing those to whom the norm is addressed to respect it. And yet, the analysis carried out in the preceding lines in relation to this aspect of things, bears clear witness to the fact that, in practice, such sanctions are extremely rare, especially in relation to air pollution, and this is due to both endogenous and exogenous factors, as we have illustrated above.

The impact of such results on the legal level is not to be overlooked, as a rule

[98] Julien Bétaille, *les conditions juridiques de l'effectivité de la norme en droit public interne*, op. cit.

[99] Jean Rivero, *on the dissuasive effect of legal sanctions*, quoted by Julien Bétaille, *répression et effectivité de la norme environnementale*, op.cit.

[100] Hans Kelsen, *Pure Theory of Law*, 2ème ed, ch. Eisenmann, LGDJ, Bruylant, Paris, 1999, P.20

that has not been applied, or only weakly applied, ends up falling into disuse, and fails to achieve the objectives for which it was drafted by the legislator.

Continual environmental degradation will take over as a result of repression due to the applicability of the relevant texts, and once the environment is degraded, it becomes a source of various diseases.

2.2. On the health front

It has already been pointed out that air pollution has a negative impact on health, according to various World Health Organization reports.

The air we breathe is our body's fuel. It is the first element necessary for life, and breathing is a vital human function. This is how Apolline Henry tells us that air pollution is a real scourge.

Referring to a new report by the University of Chicago's Energy Police Institute, published on Tuesday June 14, 2022, it emerges that 97.3% of the world's population lives in an area where air pollution exceeds the levels recommended by the World Health Organization. This figure is constantly evolving: in 2004, the WHO indicated that 92% of the world's population breathed air that was too polluted; air pollution was already particularly worrying in Asia (China, India, etc.), Africa (Congo, Cameroon, Egypt, etc.) and South America (Peru, Honduras, etc.) . [101]

Medical studies provide ample evidence of the negative impact of air pollution on human health, caused by polluting particles suspended in the ambient air. In this respect, the figures are staggering. For example, between 2016 and 2019, air pollution caused 40,000 deaths a year in France. In France, air pollution (and, in particular, fine pesticides) was responsible for 7% of annual mortality, and reduced the life expectancy of those exposed to it by an average of 8 months.

In Europe, the situation is even more frightening. According to a report by the European Environment Agency (EEA) published in October 2018, almost 500,000 Europeans die every year from overexposure to air pollutants. And worldwide, air pollution is said to reduce overall life expectancy by an average of two years, rising to 10 years in some countries such as Asia.

The causal link between exposure to air pollution and mortality is now well established, explain the experts at Santé Publique France. Air pollutants have a pro-

[101] Apolline Henry, note available at: https://www.topssnte.com/medecine/environnment-et- sante/pollution-de-l-air-causes-sante-643602 [accessed July 13, 2022]

inflammatory action at cellular level: they are responsible for oxidative stress, which promotes inflammation in the body, r e s u l t i n g in a concrete impact at cellular level, especially on the cardiovascular and respiratory systems . [102]

Indeed, the African Studies Group coordinated by Catherine Liousse and Sylvia Becerra reports that the circulation of air pollution in Africa merits urgent attention. Concentration levels of certain atmospheric pollutants far exceed the standards recommended by the WHO, and are one of the main causes of death on the continent, with an estimated o n e million deaths per year.

This situation is linked first and foremost to the flow of pollutants emitted by anthropogenic sources (domestic and commercial activities, traffic, waste combustion, industry, thermal power stations, road dust), but also those linked to agriculture and bush fires (savannah). Most are unregulated and few are monitored.

In addition to these anthropogenic sources, there are natural sources such as dust from African deserts and biogenic emissions from soils and vegetation. Variations in the circulation of these pollutant flows across the continent are subject to meteorological factors, which determine their seasonal intensity . [103]

In addition, current climatic upheavals are having an impact on these factors, as well as on the flows of certain emission sources, and vice versa. The circulation of air pollution is therefore highly uneven in its spatial and temporal distribution, but it is also socially uneven, with the most vulnerable people subject to the heaviest pollution. These vulnerabilities are also on the move, as they can circulate between social categories or spread differently depending on location, aggregating with other vulnerabilities and even propagating over time . [104]

If the situation is critical today, what will it be tomorrow? Africa's population is expected to reach 2 billion by 2040, with a world record urban density rate. If no measures are taken to reduce emissions between now and then, the flow of pollutants and the resulting air pollution will explode.

It follows from the above analysis that the ineffectiveness and inefficiency of air pollution control mechanisms in the EIS are detrimental to the environment. So it's not enough to enshrine certain values in conventions, treaties, directives or constitutions in order to produce magical effects without any other action being taken in this

[102] Idem

[103] Studies conducted by the Groupement d'intérêt scientifique (GIS) "études africaines en France", session A56, available at: https://etudes-africaines.cnrs.fr/les-rencontres-du-gis/circulation-de-la-pollution-de- lair-en-afrique/

[104] Idem

direction. There must also be action to be taken, and this action must be dissuasive and binding.

According to Maurice Kamto, environmental law is not yet sufficiently conceived in Africa as the product of a decision by Africans to meet local requirements.

It is not perceived as the normative translation of an endogenous, conscious and deliberate national policy for the protection of nature and the sustainable management of natural resources and spaces for present and future generations. Like the protection of human rights, environmental law is still regarded in many African countries as an extreme constraint that must be complied with out of necessity.

Admittedly, progress in this area has been more or less remarkable, depending on the country. But, on the whole, this conception persists, all the more so as environmental requirements are still seen by some as an obstacle to the economic emergence of countries . [105]

So, if we are to claim that the mechanisms for repressing air pollution in EIA are truly effective, and avoid the unfortunate consequences that result, both institutional and normative reform are essential. This justifies our examination of the following point, through which we will put forward our suggestions for remedying the problem of low effectiveness.

[105] Maurice Kamto, *la mise en œuvre du droit de l'environnement : forces et faiblesses des cadres institutionnels*, in Revue Africaine du droit international de l'environnement, n° 1, 2014, PP.29-36

CHAPTER 2. FUTURE PROSPECTS

In the light of the analysis carried out in the preceding lines, it follows that there is a need to strengthen air pollution enforcement mechanisms with a view to achieving real effectiveness (section 1). Environmental protection is, moreover, an individual right. It is even a fundamental right. This raises the question, as René Cassin did, of how individuals, as holders of these rights, can be given the legal means to ensure that States respect their obligations in this area.

It's true that certain guarantees already exist at both universal (international) and regional levels. On a regional level, we have, in fact, noted the CJEU, not forgetting the African Court of Human and Peoples' Rights.

However, as we have seen, these guarantees are not very effective in settling disputes relating to air pollution in particular. We must therefore consider the evolutionary dynamics of a legal framework for the repression of air pollution in EIS (section 2). It is in this light that we could claim to be effectively combating air pollution.

Section 1. THE NEED TO REINFORCE THE EFFECTIVENESS OF AIR POLLUTION CONTROL MECHANISMS IN DIE

The treatment of the present work and the analysis as discussed above make it necessary to reinforce the effectiveness of the mechanisms for repressing air pollution in DIE. This is also based on the understanding of the rule of law. The need to ensure compliance with environmental protection rules derives above all from general constraints linked to the rule of law. The rule of law is characterized by the primacy of the rule of law, which is binding on all players in society.

This reinforcement rests on a foundation (§.1.) which even expresses the sense of a systemic eco-safeguard (§.2). It makes sense, therefore, first of all to present the basis for this reinforcement.

§.1. Basis for reinforcement

To present the rationale is to answer the question: why is it necessary to reinforce the effectiveness of air pollution control mechanisms? Or, alternatively, what are the main reasons why such reinforcement is necessary?

The ineffectiveness of a rule of law constitutes a factor of insecurity for citizens and a serious threat to the reality of the rule of law. In environmental matters, ineffectiveness or lack of effectiveness paves the way for all kinds of abuse and human-induced environmental degradation.

The law aims to organize society, to regulate and order social relations. As such, it guarantees citizens effective protection. However, the ineffectiveness of the law leaves the individual free to act as he wishes, without any constraints. The result is what is known as the law of the jungle, i .e. the rule of the strongest, with the consequence that the individual, left to his or her own devices and unprotected, lives in total legal insecurity.

The ineffectiveness or weak effectiveness of the law, through the uncertainty it creates with regard to the law, risks undermining justice and jeopardizing the rule of law, which is the very essence of any democratic society[106] . According to Frank Baron, the rule of law is an institutional system in which public power is subject to the law . [107]

Moreover, this notion, of German origin (Rechtsstaat), was redefined at the beginning of the twentieth century by the Austrian jurist Hans Kelsen, as a state in which legal norms are hierarchized in such a way as to limit its power. The existence of a hierarchy of norms is one of the most important guarantees of the rule of law. Within this framework, the competences of the various organs of the State are precisely defined, and the norms they enact are only valid on condition that they respect all the higher legal norms. At the top of this pyramid is the constitution, followed by international commitments, laws and regulations . [108]

This legal structure is binding on all legal entities. The State, which has the power to enact law, is itself subject to legal rules, whose regulatory function is thus affirmed and legitimized. The equality of legal subjects and the independence of the judiciary are conditions for the existence of a state governed by the rule of law.

For the latter, and in order to have any practical effect, the principle of the rule of law presupposes the existence of independent jurisdictions, competent to settle disputes between different legal persons in application of the principle of legality, which derives from the existence of the hierarchy of norms, and the principle of

[106] Laurent Granier, op.cit, P.28
[107] Frank Baron, note available at: https://www.vie-publique.fr/parole-dexpert/270286-quest-ce- que-letat-de-droit [consulted on July 21, 2022]
[108] Note available at: https://www.vie-publique.fr/parole-dexpert/270286-quest-ce-que-letat-de- droit [consulted on July 21, 2022]

equality, which is opposed to any differentiated treatment of legal persons. Such a model implies the existence of a separation of powers and an independent judiciary.

The rule of law is above all a theoretical model. But it has also become a political theme, since it is now considered to be the main feature of democratic regimes. By making law a privileged instrument for regulating political and social organization, it subordinates the principle of legitimacy to respect for legality. It thus justifies the growing role of the courts in countries that claim to follow this model . [109]

In the particular or specific field of environmental law, the ineffectiveness of the law results not only in the paralysis of the rule of law, but also in the development of ecological incivism and other practices favoring environmental degradation . [110]

Etienne Cerexhe, quoted by Laurent Granier, emphasizes that "*the rule of law is a sun that never sets, whose rays must light us up eternally*". Moreover, international environmental law is a rising sun that may never shine if it remains a dead letter. As we have certainly seen above, the jurisdictional mechanism set up to punish air pollution is not very effective, for the various reasons mentioned.

Thus, international environmental law must be seen as an instrument capable of contributing to the achievement of sustainable development objectives, while aiming to bring about an effective change in people's behaviour towards the environment in general and, in particular, towards the preservation of air quality, while forcing them to adopt a more rational and respectful attitude towards the various elements that make up it.

Indeed, reinforcing the effectiveness of air pollution control mechanisms is also a way of guarding against dangerous human attitudes, whose non-observance could pave the way for any deterioration in air quality. Sustainable development, the rule of law and the effectiveness of the aforementioned repressive mechanisms can only be achieved if the rules protecting the environment are respected. Reinforcing the effectiveness of these mechanisms means fighting effectively and efficiently to eradicate any damage that may result.

Charlotte LEPITRE points out that, although air pollution is recognized as a real social issue and a health and environmental risk, there are still many points to be strengthened in order to reduce this threat. Starting with monitoring, which enables us to identify pollutants and sources of emissions, which in turn guides research, but

---

[109] Idem

[110] Laurent Granier, op.cit. P.28

also communication and action . [111]

Indeed, she continues, there is a strong need to strengthen information. In her opinion, providing the right information and reading keys adapted to the target audience not only raises awareness, but also encourages action . [112]

When we are faced with a threat, the main objective is to eliminate it, or at least to reduce it by the source of emission or exposure. And while air pollution is an omnipresent threat throughout the world, even if it is often invisible and its costs hidden, the reality of its consequences is undeniable . [113]

If monitoring and information systems are strengthened, and the various players involved demonstrate a firm commitment, a genuine policy to reduce air pollution cannot fail[114] . The means of reinforcing this effectiveness will be developed further below.

§.2. Eco-systemic safeguards

Global economic performance is rising steadily with the increase in world population and the desire to achieve the highest standard of living, coupled with growing global connectivity and technological and scientific advances. The result is a growing anthropogenic impact on the biosphere as a whole, making environmental protection all the more important. Environmental protection therefore refers to all measures for the ecological protection of biotopes, in order to maintain human health . [115]

Polluters should take responsibility for environmental management and should not be used to their own advantage. Environmental protection focuses on different parts of the natural environment, including air, soil, water and climate. Thus, the starting point of environmental protection is the preservation of people's living environment and health. This includes, to a certain extent, the protection of human nature . [116]

The latter (ecosystem) is an assembly of animals, plants and micro-organisms

---

[111] Charlotte LEPITRE, *les points à renforcer en matière de lutte contre la pollution de l'air*, in Annales des Mines, Responsabilités & environnement, la pollution de l'air, série trimestrielle n° 96, Paris cedex, octobre 2019, P.22
[112] Idem
[113] Daniel CALLEJA CRESPO, *politiques publiques européennes*, in Annales des Mines, Responsabilité & environnement, la pollution de l'air, série trimestrielle n° 96, Paris Cedex 12, octobre 2019, P.26
[114] Charlotte LEPITRE, op.cit, P.22
[115] This definition of environmental protection is available at: https://www.aquaportail.com/definition-14345-protection-de-l-environnement.html
[116] Idem

interacting with each other and with their environment. Or better still, it is an ensemble formed by a specific community of living beings, such as plants, animals and micro-organisms (biocenosis), and a given space (biotope), which interact as a functional unit. Thanks to these interactions between the environment and the species, as well as the interactions between the species themselves, a biological and ecological equilibrium is established.

These interactions take place in systems that are more or less natural: forest, agricultural, urban [...] Man participates in these interactions, on which his health and well-being depend . [117]

It follows that ecosystems provide services that are essential to the development of human societies. They clean the air we breathe and the water we drink; they control the proliferation of pathogenic organisms; and they renew soil fertility . [118]

Ecosystems deserve enormous protection, because the impacts of air pollution are devastating. The first United Nations Conference on the Human Environment, held in Stockholm in 1972, paid particular attention to this issue.

New evidence of lake acidification in Sweden was presented in a case study entitled *"Air pollution beyond national borders. The environmental impact of sulfur in air and precipitation".* Atmospheric deposition of sulfur has also been blamed for forest dieback in Germany and Scandinavia. At European level, the fight against this type of pollution was organized within the Geneva Convention on Transboundary Air Pollution, now known as the Air Convention, set up in 1979 . [119]

It was within this framework that the concept of critical loads was developed. It is designed to establish maximum acceptable levels of atmospheric pollutant deposition for each type of ecosystem. Returning to the Air Convention, the latter has also set up networks for monitoring the effects of pollution on ecosystems, making it possible to confirm the diagnoses made by forecasting the exceedance of critical loads and to monitor the impact of the emission reduction measures implemented.

It should be noted that the critical load concept has thus enabled the development of emission reduction policies, such as the 1985 Helsinki Sulphur

---

[117] Henry Décamps, *les écosystèmes*, Institut de France Académie des sciences, livret sur l'environnement, 2020, available online at: https://www.academie-sciences.fr/pdf/rapport/livret_6.pdf

[118] Idem

[119] Eva LEOZ-GARZIANDIA, *les impacts de la pollution de l'air*, in Annales des mines, Responsabilité & environnement, la pollution de l'air, op.cit, P.11

Protocol or the multi-pollutant, multi-effect Gothenburg Protocol adopted in 1999 and revised in 2012, which targets, in its amended version, ozone, fine particles and acidifying and eutrophying pollutants . [120]

Hence, the disruption of this eco-systemic balance, even if it affects a single organism, can result in very significant (considerable) and irreversible damage. Human beings, like all living beings, are part of ecosystems. Ecosystems are the main supports of human life, from which we derive not only food, but also all the resources found in our physical environment and used to satisfy our needs.

Man has always interacted with and benefited from ecosystems, but the problem arises when he begins to overexploit them, significantly modifying and destroying them, and thereby destabilizing them. Today, human beings are the main threat to ecosystems, jeopardizing their very existence. The speed at which mankind modifies nature does not give it time to regenerate . [121]

And yet, as we have just pointed out, in ecosystems there are interactions between species and the environment, and between different species (interspecific relationships), as well as between members of each species (intra-specific relationships), establishing a biological equilibrium. This means that the existence of one species conditions the existence of another, and influences the proper functioning of the environment.

The ecosystem, or more precisely the natural or physical environment, is the main promoter of this equilibrium, as it provides the appropriate conditions for interactions between the environment and species, and between the species themselves. If the food chain breaks down due to the extinction of a species, the ecosystem becomes unbalanced, with a detrimental effect on its biological diversity.

Consequently, an ecosystem in equilibrium makes possible the existence of a high level of biodiversity, since species, both animal and plant and other types, have a habitat in suitable conditions in which to live, and a food source for the necessary supply of organic matter, or in the case of plants, inorganic matter.

Ecosystem conservation is of course based on the fact that ecosystems are essential to the existence of all life on earth, since they provide a large number of goods and services.

---

[120] Idem

[121] Sandra Ropero Portillo, *Ecosystems - importance and preservation*, article available at: https://www.projetecolo.com/les-ecosystemes-importance-et-preservation-177.html#anchor_2 [accessed July 27, 2022]

Ensuring the natural equilibrium of all types of ecosystems is vital if nature is to continue its course, but for many years they have been seriously affected by human intervention . [122]

This eco-systemic safeguard can also prevent the acceleration of climate change and the rise of social conflicts due to the scarcity of goods, such as water due to the disappearance of aquifers, or food due to the loss of soil fertility. Secondly, their protection continues to improve people's health and prevent the proliferation of new diseases. It also guarantees a favorable environment for future generations.

A degraded environment in no way guarantees life expectancy, and becomes the cause or source of death. Indeed, as Antoine Decrouy points out, environmental degradation is the loss of the environment's capacity to satisfy the earth's social, biodiversity and environmental needs. Environmental degradation occurs when the earth's natural resources are depleted or damaged, and the environment is compromised . [123]

The consequences of environmental degradation are varied, and can include species extinction, loss of biodiversity, poor air quality, water pollution, soil erosion and an increase in the greenhouse effect. Although many of these effects are not visible in the short term, they are visible in the long term.

This is why current actions can have an impact on future environmental degradation[124] . Hence the wisdom of safeguarding the ecosystem by combating any degradation it may face, in order to aim for sustainable living patterns.

This can only be achieved by adopting means (measures) to reinforce the effectiveness of repressive mechanisms. This justifies the following section.

---

[122] Idem

[123] Antoine Decruy, Environmental degradation: definition, causes and consequences, article available at: https://www.projetecolo.com/degradation-de-l-environnement-definition-causes-et-consequences- 108.html [consulted on July 27, 2022]

[124] Idem

Section 2. TOWARDS A DYNAMIC EVOLUTION OF A LEGAL FRAMEWORK FOR THE REPRESSION OF AIR POLLUTION IN DIE

An examination of the existing legal framework for the repression of air pollution, as presented above, reveals a number of weaknesses. These weaknesses are both normative and institutional.

The deficiency of this normative and jurisdictional aspect of the repression of air pollution should be remedied by the reform of this legal framework through the adoption of a universal binding legal instrument (§1) on the one hand, and by the implementation of new institutions to monitor violations of international air pollution law (§2) on the other.

§.1. Adoption of a universal, binding legal instrument

According to Paul Amselek, legal rules are tools for the public direction of human conduct, tools of command or public government, with law fulfilling a public direction function . [125]

In a way, this steering function is consubstantial with the law, and is directly linked to its relationship with the fact. As a political instrument, the law seeks, with varying degrees of success, to ensure that the fact conforms to the rule . [126]

Indeed, these rules serve as an instrument for resolving any disputes that may arise between parties. Environmental litigation can be understood as all disputes arising from the application of environmental protection rules. It may take place before either the administrative or the judicial courts, depending on the parties to the dispute and its subject matter . [127]

It therefore follows that there is a need to adopt a universal binding legal instrument in the field of air pollution protection.

[125] Paul AMSELEK, *le droit, technique de direction publique des conduites humaines*, Droits, n° 10, 1989, P.10, quoted by julien Bétaille, Thèse, les conditions juridiques de l'effectivité de la norme en droit public interne : illustration en droit de l'urbanisme et en droit de l'environnement, University of Limoges, December 2012, P.8

[126] François TERRE, *forces et faiblesses de la norme*, in Catherine THIBIERGEGE et alii, la force normative, naissance d'un concept, LGDJ- Bruylant, Paris, 2009, P.9

[127] Emmanuel D. Kam Yogo, op. cit. P. 171

And the advent of this international legal instrument of universal scope on air protection should at the same time determine the legal regime applicable in this field. Indeed, there is no general convention on the international responsibility of the State in environmental matters, even though there are a number of specific conventions.

The consequence of this absence, or lack of existence, of a general system of international liability in environmental matters is that the classic rules of public international law have to be applied. This absence is also subject to one of the weaknesses and, as we have seen above, these weaknesses have the negative effect of weakening the effectiveness of air pollution enforcement mechanisms.

However, the situation seems to be tempered at European regional level. The Lugano Convention on Civil Liability for Damage resulting from Activities Dangerous to the Environment, adopted in June 1993 by the Council of Europe, is based on the "polluter pays" principle. In particular, this convention requires industrial groups to participate in a financial security scheme (article 12), for example by taking out an insurance policy to cover the risks arising from their environmentally hazardous activities . [128]

The Lugano Convention is a regional implementation of the 1992 Rio Declaration on Environment and Development, Principle 13 of which stipulates that States must draw up legislation on liability for pollution and other environmental damage, and on compensation for victims. To this end, the most important dispute before the Luxembourg Court concerned the poor transposition, failure to transpose or delay in transposing numerous European environmental directives (water, air, habitats, waste, GMOs, etc.) into the domestic law of member states.

In this very particular case, the State is clearly in breach of its obligations, and is exposed to proceedings brought by a very determined European Commission (particularly alerted by complaints from individuals and their groups, or on its own initiative) before the European courts for failure to fulfil its obligation to transpose . [129]

Séverine NADAUD also points out in this respect that failure to comply leads to

---

[128] Séverine NADAUD, la responsabilité internationale en matière d'environnement, op.cit, P.8

[129] Idem

very substantial and, to say the least, dissuasive financial penalties (fines, periodic penalty payments).

The codification of a worldwide binding legal instrument on air protection will certainly have the necessary effectiveness to halt the deterioration in air quality, because of the constraint that the said instrument will organize. In the absence of a binding global legal instrument on air protection, the deterioration of air quality worldwide could be perpetuated in a very worrying way.

In view of the real need to protect the environment in general, and air pollution in particular, it would be wise to codify this instrument as a matter of urgency, in order to make protective measures more effective in this sector, particularly air pollution.

This dynamic evolution of the legal framework for the suppression of air pollution in the EIS, through the adoption of this binding instrument of worldwide scope, must move on to the realm of positivism. For the purpose of the rule of law, or the aim of a rule of law, is to ensure order in a society through its prescriptions. This purpose is achieved through the effective application of the said rule by bodies legally instituted for this purpose.

Hence the reason for the development of the following point.

§.2. Implementing new institutions to monitor violations of international air pollution law and ensure its effectiveness

The implementation of new control institutions is essential if the binding international legal instrument on air protection is to be effective. This institutional control mechanism can be divided into two categories: The non-jurisdictional institutional mechanism and the jurisdictional mechanism.

This duality of control mechanisms is based on the need to respect and sanction non-compliance with environmental protection rules in general, and air pollution in particular.

2.1. In a non-jurisdictional context

Professor Bénédicte Delaunay takes the view that non-jurisdictional protections are guarantees designed to defend rights by non-jurisdictional means, i.e.

outside the judicial function of the courts . [130]

For MATADI NENGA GAMANDA, non-jurisdictional dispute resolution mechanisms are understood to mean mechanisms other than trial courts for settling disputes. These include conciliation, mediation and arbitration. The combination of these three modes, he says, gives rise to composite formulas that can be found here and there . [131]

Taken in this non-jurisdictional framework, these bodies will play a vital role in protecting air quality, based on better techniques than those of the reports instituted or set up by the EIS. It has to be said that reporting techniques have serious practical limitations.

On the one hand, there is the problem of the very quality of the reports drawn up by the States, and on the other, the delay in the processing of these reports by the committees, which is one of the limitations that can be noted.

This new non-jurisdictional mechanism will be made up of experts who have a real grasp of the situation in the countries where they will be exercising their function, and who will also have to maximize the sense of effective follow-up by monitoring the standard. And in terms of techniques, the body or, better still, the committee thus set up will be able to use mainly the technique known as "surveillance".

That, in the event of non-compliance with environmental rules designed to protect air quality, there should be effective repression of those responsible for violating the said rules. This would prevent legal instruments adopted in this way from falling into disuse. This system would obviously avoid any strategy of support not only for the defaulting State, but also for any other public or private legal entity guilty of violating the aforementioned rules, by of course holding them accountable.

This direct consequence of the system involves classic liability, based on the sanctioning of violations of the international legal instrument on air protection. This compliance will exercise a systematic and vigorous control with the aim of preserving air quality.

---

[130] B. Delaunay, *les protections non juridictionnelles des droits subjectifs des administrés*, quoted by Dimitri LÖHRE, *la protection non juridictionnelle des droits fondamentaux en droit constitutionnel comparé, l'exemple de l'ombudsman spécialise portugais, Espagnol et Français*, Thesis, Université de Pau et des Pays de L'ADOUR, June 2013, P.24

[131] MATADI NENGA GAMANDA, la question du pouvoir judiciaire en République Démocratique du Congo, contribution à une théorie de réforme, édition Droit et idées nouvelles, Kinshasa, 2001, P.278

It should also be noted that, in practical terms, the law of liability has not yet been developed, with the result that most disputes between states have been settled by negotiation, as opposed to the judicial settlement of disputes.

And yet, it has to be said that this method of dispute settlement (jurisdictional) offers considerable advantages. The developments that follow will demonstrate this.

2.2. In a jurisdictional context

Sanction, in its negative sense, is the harm inflicted on a person as a consequence of an act contrary to the law[132] . Thus, to speak of a sanction, there must necessarily be the effective and operational existence of a judicial body set up for this purpose.

Indeed, in order to protect the environment and, more specifically, air quality, judicial review is the culmination of the implementation of legal instruments adopted in this field. In this respect, the study carried out in the preceding lines has revealed the non-existence of a World Court or an international environmental jurisdiction to centralize disputes in this field. And this constitutes one of the weaknesses in the effectiveness of air pollution repression .

It would be desirable to set up a specific world jurisdiction to centralize all disputes arising from the violation of environmental protection rules. In contrast to the ICJ, and with a view to reinforcing the effectiveness of the repression of air pollution as well as the applicability of the related legal instrument on a universal scale, and to give the latitude to legal entities under private law to be able to seize this judicial body with a view to asserting their claims. This possibility can also be extended to private individuals and non-governmental organizations.

Human beings (individuals) are part of nature, and human rights are closely linked to the environment in which we live. Environmental damage hinders the enjoyment of human rights and, conversely, the exercise of human rights helps to protect the environment and promote sustainable development.

A safe, clean, healthy and sustainable environment is necessary for the full enjoyment of human rights, including the right to life, the right to the highest attainable standard of physical and mental health, the right to an adequate standard of living,

[132] J.H.ROBERT, *Droit pénal général*, Paris, PUF, 6(eme) édition, 2005, P.54 quoted by Amandine chouvet-Lefrançois, "*Les finalités de la sanction en droit pénal*", available at: https://books.openedition.org/putc/1778?lang=fr

the right to adequate food, the right to safe drinking water and sanitation, the right to clean air, the right to development and the right to a healthy environment, which i s enshrined in regional agreements and most national constitutions . [133]

Moreover, as the report by the Club des Juristes points out, individuals are directly concerned by international environmental standards, since these help to guarantee an individual right which belongs to them and which they can demand to be respected: the right to a healthy environment[134] . And yet, with the International Court of Justice (ICJ), there is no way in which individuals can claim to have recourse to it.

Furthermore, we believe that this World Court of the Environment could rule in the first and last instance on all disputes between parties within the continental area different in terms of geographical location. On the other hand, the aforementioned Court would rule in the last resort for all disputes whose appeal level has been emptied by the regional environmental Court of the parties to the proceedings.

So much so that at every regional level (on every continent), Regional Environmental Courts (RECs) should exist and be operational, their jurisdiction being mutatis mutandis that of the World Environmental Court (WEC) at regional level.

In effect, the Regional Environmental Court (REC) would rule at first and second instance on disputes between parties belonging to the same region. In other words, disputes arising within the same region.

In addition, the CRE would rule in the final instance, i.e. in cassation, on all disputes that the domestic courts had settled on appeal.

In our view, this jurisdictional mechanism for controlling violations of environmental protection rules would deliver effective results in the fight against air quality degradation.

It is certainly true that a significant advance has been made at European regional level with the existence of environmental tribunals. The same is true of the legal framework governing the environment. On this issue, Séverine NADAUD clearly

---

133 Notes enshrined in the Convention on Access to Information, Public Participation in Decision-Making and Access to Justice in Environmental Matters, art 1; the African Charter on Human and Peoples' Rights, art 24; the Additional Protocol to the American Convention on Human Rights in the Area of Economic, Social and Cultural Rights, art 11;

134 Rapport du club des juristes, op.cit. p.22

underlines that in European Union law, state obligations relating to environmental protection are numerous and derive from both primary and secondary legislation . [135]

However, we believe that the ideal situation would be for these environmental jurisdictions to become effective and operational throughout the rest of the continent, with dissuasive decisions designed to produce effects on the ground. With the advent of these specialized (environmental) jurisdictions, the ICJ will lose all material jurisdiction over environmental litigation. At least, it (the ICJ) remains to this day the only principal jurisdiction of the United Nations with a general competence, and it is only because of the absence of the said specialized jurisdiction that the ICJ has been given this competence.

Some authors, like Bruce, suggest that this future jurisdiction should be able to impose sanctions according to the nature of the infringement, ranging from the payment of damages, punitive damages, to the restoration of the site and rehabilitation of the damaged habitat in cases where this is still possible.

It also suggests that fines and prison sentences be envisaged for environmental crimes . [136]

From this perspective, we are convinced that the advent and operationalization of these mechanisms could serve as a lever on which to build a sustainable development of the EIS, with the positive consequence of the effectiveness and efficiency of air pollution repression mechanisms.

In this way, the fight against the deterioration of air quality will be effective, and we will be able to live in a healthy, propitious and unpolluted environment thanks to this institutional and legal reform of the EIS.

---

[135] Séverine NADAUD underlines this point in her course module entitled International environmental responsibility on page 8, option 1 international environmental law, University of Limoges, op.cit,

[136] Bruce, quoted by Marina Isabelle BAMBARA ZONGO, vers le pacte mondial pour l'environnement, Master 2 Droit international de l'environnement thesis, University of Limoges, August 2021, P.106

CONCLUSION

The study of air pollution control mechanisms in the DIE has enabled us to reflect in depth on the impact that these mechanisms as set up by the DIE represent in relation to air protection through their application. It's clear that the EIS is designed to protect sustainable development by safeguarding the environment and the ecosystem as a whole.

The issue of air pollution and ecosystem degradation is becoming increasingly worrying at both universal and regional levels. The use of natural resources by developed countries and the impact of this development have immense and unfortunate repercussions on the environment in general.

Bearing in mind the risks to natural resources and air, a number of non-binding measures to protect them are scattered throughout a number of texts (conventions, directives, etc.).

In other words, as Romain Melot and Hai Vu Pham also point out, many environmental risk assessments deplore the inadequacy of preventive control, curative measures and sanctions against those responsible for pollution and nuisance . [137]

Faced with this deficient and ineffective picture of the repression of air pollution in international environmental law, international diplomacy will have to be active in order to militate in favor of this renewal of the effectiveness of the said mechanisms, for there is no doubt that environmental disasters transcend borders, and the resulting damage is so immense.

In its fight to curb air pollution, the EIS needs to equip itself with a binding and dissuasive instrument as a standard for regulating international life.

The challenge is certainly not only to revise the EIS legal framework by adopting a binding legal instrument of universal scope for air protection, but also and above all to implement it effectively in order to achieve efficient results.

---

[137] Romain Melot and Vu Pham, *Protection de l'environnement et stratégies contentieuses. Une étude du recours à la justice administrative*, éditions juridiques, droit et société, 2012/3 n°82, P.621 - 641, article available online at: https://www.cairn.info/revue-droit-et-societe1-2012-3-page-621.htm

This reform of the EID's legal framework, resulting in the creation of a specialized international jurisdiction (CME) in the matter, with the renewed interventionism of other players (NGOs, individuals and legal entities under private or non-state law) to be able to appear before the latter, will thus enable the EID to fight effectively against any attempt at environmental degradation. It is within this framework, as described above in terms of perspectives, that the mechanisms for repressing air pollution will be effective and efficient in DIE.

BIBLIOGRAPHY

1. Official texts

- Agenda 21;
- 1972 Stockholm Declaration on the Human Environment;
- 1992 Rio Declaration;
- World Declaration on the Environmental Rule of Law adopted in Rio de Janeiro on April 29, 2016 ;
- African Charter on Human and Peoples' Rights, 1981;
- United Nations Framework Convention on Climate Change of May 9, 1992, which entered into force on March 21, 1994;
- Stockholm Convention on Persistent Organic Pollutants of May 22, 2001;
- African Convention on the Conservation of Nature, July 11, 2003;
- Bamako Convention on the Ban of the Import into Africa of Hazardous Wastes and on the Control of Transboundary Movements and Management of Hazardous Wastes within Africa of January 30, 1991;
- Directive (EU) 2015/2193 of the European Parliament and of the Council of November 25, 2015 on the limitation of emissions of certain pollutants into the air from average combustion plants;
- Directive 2002/3/C of February 12, 2002 of the European Parliament and of the Council relating to ozone in ambient air;
- Directive 2008/50 of May 21, 2008 on air quality;
- Loi N° 11/009 du 09 Juillet 2011 Portant principes fondamentaux relatifs à la protection de l'environnement en République Démocratique du Congo;
- Loi N° 98- 030 du 12 Février 1998 portant loi-cadre sur l'environnement en République du Bénin ;
- Law N° 96/12 of August 5, 1996 on the framework law for environmental management in Cameroon;
- Law No. 2008-005 of May 30, 2008 on the framework law on the environment in Togo;
- Protocol to the Espo Convention on Environmental Impact Assessment in a Transboundary Context on Strategic Environmental Assessment of May 21, 2003, which entered into force on July 11, 2010;
- Kyoto Protocol of February 16, 2005;

- Additional Protocol to the American Convention on Human Rights in the Area of Economic, Social and Cultural Rights of November 17, 1988, entered into force November 16, 1999;
- Protocol on the Financing of the Cooperative Programme for Monitoring and Evaluation of the Long-range Transmission of Air Pollutants of September 28, 1984;
- Protocol on the reduction of sulphur emissions or their transboundary fluxes by at least 30% of July 08, 1985;
- Protocol concerning the Control of Emissions of Nitrogen Oxides or their Transboundary Fluxes of October 31, 1988;
- Protocol concerning the control of emissions of volatile organic compounds or their transboundary fluxes of November 18, 1991;
- Protocol on Further Reduction of Sulphur Emissions of June 14, 1994;
- Protocol on Heavy Metals of June 24, 1998 ;
- Protocol on Persistent Organic Pollutants of June 24, 1998;
- Protocol to Abate Acidification, Eutrophication and Ground-level Ozone of November 30, 1999;
- Regulation (EU) 2019/631 of the European Parliament and of the Council of 17 April 2019 setting emission performance standards for $C0_2$for new passenger cars and light-duty vehicles and repealing Regulations /EC/N°443/2009 and /EC/N°510/2011 ;
- Statute of the ICJ.

2. WORKS

- Aser NZOVU LUVUJI, Constitutionalisation du droit de l'eau et souveraineté des Etats: contribution pour une meilleure protection des ressources en eau, European University Publishing, 2017 ;
- Aser NZOVU LUVUJI, les techniques juridiques de la prévention de la pollution de l'eau, éditions universitaires européennes, 2018, 259 Pages;
- Proceedings of the seminar organized by the CSR (Corporate Social Responsibility) platform under the theme: the role of law in environmental protection, September 2018;
- Auguste MAMPUYA KANUNK'A - TSHIAPO, Traité de droit international public, médiaspaul, Kinshasa, 2016 ;
- François TERRE, Forces et faiblesses de la norme, in Catherine THIBIERGEGE et alii, force normative, naissance d'un concept, LGDJ, Bruylant, paris, 2009 ;
- Emmanuel D. KAN YOGO, Manuel judiciaire de droit de l'environnement en Afrique, Québec, IFFD, 2018, 236 Pages;
- G. KALAMBAY LUMPUNGU and PAULIN MUNENE YAMBA - YAMBA, droit Congolais de l'environnement, édition Espérance, Paris, 2020 ;
- Hans KELSEN, Pure Theory of Law, 2nd edition, ch.Eisenman, LGDJ, Bruylant, Paris, 1999;
- J.H. ROBERT, Droit pénal Général, Paris, PUF, 6^{eme}edition, 2005;
- Jean-Pierre BEURIER, droit international de l'environnement, ed. Pedone, 2017;
- Jacqueline MAURAND-DEVILLER, le droit de l'environnement, Presses universitaires de France, 2015;
- John RAWLS, Theory of Justice, Threshold, Paris, 1997;
- KISS ALENDRE, la convention sur la pollution atmosphérique transfrontière à longue distance, Revue juridique de l'environnement, n 1, 1985 ;
- Laurent GRANIER, (coord), Aspects contemporains du droit de l'environnement en Afrique de l'Ouest et Centrale, IUCN, Gland, Switzerland. Xvi, 2008, 224 Pages;
- Mario BETTATI, le droit international de l'environnement, Odile Jacob, 2012, 304 Pages;

- Maurice KAMTO, environmental law in Africa, Paris, Edicef/AUPELF, 1996;
- Maurice KAMTO, la mise en œuvre du droit de l'environnement : forces et faiblesses des cadres institutionnels, in Revue Africaine du droit international de l'environnement, n° 1, 2014 ;
- MATADI NENGA GAMANDA, la question du pouvoir judiciaire en République Démocratique du Congo, contribution à une théorie de réforme, ed. Droit et idées nouvelles, Kinshasa, 2001, 530 Pages;
- Michel COUTOU, Max Weber et les rationalités du droit, LGDJ, Paris, 1995;
- Michel PRIEUR, les indicateurs juridiques, outils d'évaluation de l'effectivité du droit de l'environnement, Institut de la Francophonie pour le développement durable (IFFD), Quebec, 2018, 159 Pages;
- Michel PRIEUR, droit de l'environnement, droit durable, Bruylant, 2013, 1048 Pages;
- N.U., mechanisms nationaux d'élaboration des rapports et des suivis, guide pratique sur la collaboration efficace de l'Etat avec les mécanismes internationaux des droits de l'homme, new york et Genève, 2016 ;
- Nicolas de Sadeleer, les principes du pollueur-payeur, de prévention et de précaution, essai sur la genèse et la portée juridique de quelques principes du droit de l'environnement, AUPELF-UREF, Bruylant Bruxelles, 1999, 437 Pages;
- Paul REUTER, introduction au droit des traités, graduate institute publications, Geneva, 1985, 256 Pages;
- Raphael ROMI, droit et administration de l'environnement, 4th edition, Montchrestien, EJA, Paris, 2001;
- Serge GUINCHARD et alii, lexique des termes juridiques, 25th ed, Dalloz, 2017-2018 ;

3. Theses and dissertations

- Aser NZOVU LUVUJI, prevention of water pollution in the Congo Basin: Evaluation and redefinition of the regional and national mechanisms of the founding states of the International Commission of the Congo-Oubangui-Sangha Basin (CICOS), PhD thesis in law, University of Kisangani, 2019-2020 ;
- Coffi Dieudonné ASSOUVI, l'influence du droit international des changements climatiques sur le droit de l'environnement de l'Union Européenne, thesis, University of Limoges, 2018 ;
- Dimitri LÖHRE, la protection non juridictionnelle des droits fondamentaux en droit constitutionnel comparé, l'exemple de l'ombudsman spécialise Portugais, Espagnol et Français, thesis, Université de Pau et des Pays de l'ADOUR, June 2013 ;
- Julien BETAILLE, les conditions juridiques de l'effectivité de la norme en droit interne : illustrations en droit de l'urbanisme et de l'environnement, thesis, University of Limoges, 2012 ;
- Yacouba SAVADOGO, la protection communautaire de l'environnement dans le cadre de l'UEMOA : enjeu, portée et perspective, thesis, University of Limoges, 2019 ;
- Marina Isabelle BAMBARA ZONGO, vers le pacte mondial pour l'environnement, Master 2 thesis, environmental law, University of Limoges, August 2021.

4. Articles and reviews

- Antoine Decruy, Environmental degradation: definition, causes and consequences, article available at: https://www.projetecolo.com/degradation-de-l-environnement-definition-causes-et-consequences-108.html
- Amos Mauris, Criteria for critically assessing the quality of a law or equivalent instrument instrument, article available at https://www.village-justice.com/articles/criteres-evaluation-critique-qualite-une-loi-instrument-equivalent 27150.html;
- Charlotte LEPITRE, les points à renforcer en matière de lutte contre la pollution de l'air, in Annales des Mines, responsabilité& environnement, la pollution de l'air, série trimestrielle n° 96, Pris cedex, octobre 2019 ;

- Daniel CALLEJA CRESPO, politiques publiques européennes, in Annales des Mines, responsabilité& environnement, la pollution de l'air, série trimestrielle n° 96, Pris cedex, octobre 2019 ;
- Eva LEOZ-GARZIANDIA, les impacts de la pollution de l'air, in Annales des Mines, responsabilité& environnement, la pollution de l'air, série trimestrielle n° 96, Pris cedex, octobre 2019 ;
- Julien Bétaille, répression et effectivité de la norme environnementale, in revue juridique de l'environnement, 2014/HSO1 volume 39, article available: https://www.cair.info/revue-juridique-de-l-environnement-2014-HSO1-page-47.htm;
- Laurence PRAT, Droit de l'air : cadre international et communautaire, April 2004, article available at: https://www.techniques-ingenieur.fr/base-documentaire/archives-th12/archives-environnement tiagO/archives-1/droit-de-l-air-cadre-international-et-communautaire-g1510/ ;
- Leatitia Van Eeck Lourt, air pollution is responsible for 9% of deaths in France, article available atà https://www.lemonde.fr/pollution/article/2016/06/21/la-pollution-de-l-air-est- responsable-de-9-de-la-mortalite-en-France 4954518 1652666.html;
- Leroy Yann, the notion effectiveness of of law, available à at: https://www.cairn.info/revue-droit-et-societe1-2011-3-page-715.htm;
- Laidi et alii, synergie entre pollens et polluants chimiques de l'air : les risques croisés, article available: https://www.Sle.com/fr/revues/sante pub/ers/e-docs/00/01/FB/D5/ article.md ?type=text.html ;
- Revue Africaine de droit de l'environnement, la protection de l'environnement par les juridictions africaines : avancées nationales et régionales, N° 05.2020 ;
- Romain Melot and Hai Vu Pham, Protection de l'environnement et stratégies contentieuses. Une étude du recours à la justice administrative, article available online at: https://www.cairn.info/revue-droit-et-societe1- 2012-3-page-621.htm;
- Sandra Ropero Portillo, les écosystèmes-importance et préservation, article available at: https://www.projetecolo.com/les-ecosystemes- importance-and-preservation-177.html#anchor 2;

- Stéphane Mandard, Air pollution kills 7 million people a year in the world. the world, alert the WHO, article available at à https://www.lemonde.fr/planete/article/2018/05/02/la-pollution-de-l-air-tue-7- million-persons-per-year-around-the-world-alert-wHO_5293076_3244.html;

5. Reports and courses

- Rapport du club des juristes, renforcer l'effectivité du droit international de l'environnement : devoirs des Etats, droits des individus, November 2005 ;
- Report n° 60 of the French Senate, extraordinary session of 2014-2015 deposit published in the official journal, ed., of laws and decrees of July 09, 2015 ;
- Bernard DROBENKO, droit international de l'environnement, option 2, droit comparé de l'environnement, le droit Français, partie 2 : les pollutions, la lutte sectorielle : l'air, cours, université de Limoges, campus numérique, envidroit, Master 2 ;
- African Commission on Human and Peoples' Rights, n° 276/03, 49eme session, 27th activity report ;
- Jean-Marc LAVIEILLE, droit international de l'environnement, cours n°1, l'air et les climats, Master 2, Université de Limoges, campus numérique, "envidroit" ;
- Michel PRIEUR, les principes généraux du droit de l'environnement, course no. 5, University of Limoges, Master 2, digital campus, "envidroit";
- Pierre-Marie DUPUY, la responsabilité internationale en matière d'environnement, AUPELF-UREF/vidéos cope, Nancy, 1998;
- Séverine NADAUD, la responsabilité internationale d'environnement, cours n°8, option 1, université de Limoges, Master 2, campus numérique, " envidroit " ;
- Séverine NADAUD, international environmental law, waste, course no. 6, option 1, University of Limoges, Master 2, digital campus, "envidroit

6. Case law and websites

- CJEU, judgment of April 28, 2022, case under C- 286/21 Commission C. République Française ;
- CJEU, judgment of February 3, 2021, case under C- 637/18 Commission C. Hungary ;
- ECOWAS: Court of Abuja, case SERAP C. Nigeria on the occasion of the July 23, 2009 application by the NGO Socio-economic Right and Accountability project;
- Arbitral award of March 11, 1941 relating to the trail foundry case;
- The High Court of Justice of Ghana, center for public interest law and Anor vs Tema oil Refinery, lawsuit no. E12/91/07, Korbiech J ;
- www.cepil.org.gh/files/cepil;
- www.ceje.ch;
- https://www.vie-publique.fr/parole-dexpert/270286-quest-ce-que-letat-de-droit;
- https://www.aquaportail.com/definition-14345-protection-de-l-environnement.html;
- https://www.academie-sciences.fr/pdf/rapport/livret_6.pdf;
- https://www.teqoya.fr/rechauffement-climatique-pollution/;
- https://www.canada.ca/fr/environnement-changement-climate/services/pollution-atmospherique/qualite-environnement-economie/ecosysteme/effet-sol-eau.html;
- https://www.eea.europa.eu/fr/help/questions-frequemment-posees/quelles-are-the-main-sources;
- https://www.dictionnaire-juridique.com/definition/etat.php;
- https://www.vie-publique.fr/parole-dexpert/270243-quest-ce-que-letat;
- https://www.topssnte.com/medecine/environnement-et-sante/pollution-de-l-air-causes-health-643602;
- https://etudes-africaines.Cnrs.fr/les-rencontres-du-gis/circulation-de-la-pollution-de-lair-en-afrique/;
- https://books.opedition.org/putc/1778?lang=fr.

TABLE OF CONTENTS